Praise for *Collaborative Disruption*

"I've known and admired Tom Muccio for years, as a member of our company's board of directors. He's one of the most thoughtful and fun thinkers I've had the pleasure of working with over the years. If you believe 'no one of us is as smart as all of us' and you work for your people, they don't work for you, *Collaborative Disruption* is the perfect book to read and share with your team."

—Ken Blanchard, coauthor of *The New One Minute Manager* and
Simple Truths of Leadership

"It was interesting to read about something that I witnessed and knew the players. I particularly enjoyed the honest discussion about the difficulties faced by each company. Too many books make change sound easy and natural. Truth is change is hard and messy. Progress is rarely a straight line forward. In this case, P&G and Walmart were successful enough that neither needed to change in the short term. We were both going to be successful whether we changed or not, which is a danger in itself. Change is most easily achieved when faced with a crisis or at least challenging conditions. To change in good times is doubly difficult."

—Lee Scott, former CEO, Walmart

"*Collaborative Disruption* captures the origin story of what can happen when leaders ask the right questions. In this case, it was Sam Walton's visionary question of 'what could happen if our two companies thought about reaching the customer as one?' I experienced the power of this collaboration vision from three vantage points: As a member of the team, which gave me a foundation of principles the rest of my career; as founder of the first true agency partner during this early stage, where we mirrored the same principles; and in my roles at Walmart in the U.S. and in the U.K., where strategic collaboration made P&G a go-to partner for transformative ideas. Tom illustrates the core principles of leadership, culture building, thinking big, and intentional design that have produced game changing results for hundreds of companies and leaders worldwide."

—Andy Murray, founder of BigQUEST Advisory and the Customer Centric Leadership Initiative; former senior vice president of marketing for Walmart US; former chief customer officer for Asda UK; and retired founder, global chairman, and CEO of Saatchi & Saatchi X

"Tom's teachings in *Collaborative Disruption* have informed many of my leadership beliefs. For example, they led to the creation of a department of strategic partnership at the Department of Veterans Affairs that helped us overcome the access crisis of 2013 and get veterans the care they earned and needed. Tom's lessons are as applicable to the government as they are to business and in general to life. Collaborative disruptions result in better outcomes and more fun in the process."

—Honorable Robert A. McDonald, 8th Secretary of the Department of Veterans Affairs; retired chairman, president and CEO of P&G; chairman of the board of the West Point Association of Graduates

"*Collaborative Disruption* highlights perseverance, leadership and innovation to transform companies and invent new business models. Walmart and P&G figured out how to get from buyer/seller negotiation to multifunctional joint value creation by focusing on winning for the customer, winning for Walmart and winning for P&G. This transformation from negotiation to value creation for consumers, for Walmart and for P&G not only changed the industry, but continues to enable these great companies to be first and best on what's next."

—Jeff Schomburger, P&G Walmart team member (starting in 1989); president of P&G Walmart global team (2004 to 2015); P&G global sales officer (2015–2019)

"The P&G-Walmart relationship is a powerful example of what is possible in a strategic relationship when a leadership team has a clear, bold vision and a commitment to developing and sustaining a culture of helping people win at work. Reading this book will help you see how forming mutually beneficial relationships plays a vital role in building strong business results. Our team at WD-40 Company applied similar principles and philosophies over a 20-year period. We were recognized as having one of the highest employee engagement measures at 93 percent, and that delivered amazing returns for our shareholders as we expanded to 176 countries. Clearly, this story and the insights from it remain highly relevant today."

—Garry Ridge, The Culture Coach, chairman emeritus and former CEO of WD-40 Company (retired 2022)

"Tom not only captures the essence of one of the biggest transformations in retail history, but the principles that made the relationship successful. I saw those principles in action and continue to use them as a leader. They are as relevant as ever, and that's what makes this book so much more than a great history lesson."

—Dina Howell, board director and retired president and CEO, Saatchi & Saatchi X; former senior vice president, global media and brand operations, P&G

"Tom's team principles as well as his personal values not only worked at P&G and Walmart, they worked for us, too. They were scalable and timeless. What I learned from Tom guided my thinking as a consultant and leader through the years. *Collaborative Disruption* shares an inspiring story with timeless principles that can transform an organization and shape a leader."

—Dan Brokke, partner, Vision Catalyst Partners; former CEO of DaySpring (a division of Hallmark) and former president, Bethany University

"I was blessed to be part of the P&G Walmart Global Customer Team from 1989 to 2008. This experience was the highlight of my forty-year career in the industry! The learnings of this experience have built a foundation that I continue to leverage today. The stories told in this book have incredible reapplication for anyone involved in driving multi-company collaboration and delivering jointly aligned results. Incredible case study opportunities with today's college classes and industry leaders."

—Mike Graen, principal owner, Collaboration LLC

"I just finished reading *Collaborative Distribution* by Tom Muccio. Aside from reliving one of the most impactful periods of my career, I was struck by how much of what we have built at ArchPoint and my own leadership style was adopted from my time on this team. Our culture is our super-power. Collaboration across all functions and divisions is at the heart of everything we do. We challenge the status quo. And the bow-tie model is the basis of our customer engagement. Finally, treating every person the same way, valuing each person's unique perspective and opinion, and leaning in to help solve the problem of the day is the foundation of my leadership style. It all sounds very familiar . . . no surprise why!"

—Jesse Edelman, CEO, ArchPoint Group

"Tom Muccio has written an entertaining and action-oriented account and road map for one of the most value-creating relationships in business history, a success story that continues to grow today. . . . Tom's extraordinary legacy was once tactical, then strategic, and is now exponential! *Collaborative Disruption* would be a great add to every executive reading list!"?

—Sandy Douglas, CEO, United Natural Foods, Inc.; former president, Coca-Cola North America

"What separates this book from others is the immediate applicability of ideas. The concepts and stories presented are important for leaders who want to reimagine, collaborate, and reactivate their personal and professional environments."

—Robert Lorber, CEO, Lorber Kamai Consulting Group; coauthor of *Putting the One-Minute Manager to Work* and *Doing What Matters*

"Helping to design and lead the Walmart Customer Team at Procter & Gamble was definitely the highlight of my career. The opportunity to work with and learn from leaders like Tom Muccio, Sam Walton, John Pepper and other executives from both companies enabled me to succeed in my career immeasurably. I frequently use examples in courses I teach at the University of Arkansas' Sam M. Walton College of Business. And, like Tom, my experiences on the team helped me enormously in many consulting endeavors after my retirement from P&G."

—Don Bechtel, adjunct instructor at the University of Arkansas and director, Walmart Global Customer Team, P&G (retired)

"This book tells the story of the incredible success of Walmart's transformational relationship with P&G. These same principles and processes are relevant today, helping customers and suppliers bring them to life in their strategic relationships."

—Christoph Senn, codirector of the INSEAD Marketing & Sales Excellence Initiative and Adjunct Professor, INSEAD

"Tom captures the excitement, adventure, and challenges of two great companies coming together to focus on better serving their consumers and shoppers. The seeds of the work have changed how business is done and is witnessed by the many multi-functional teams now headquartered in Arkansas. What used to be a breakthrough idea is now standard operating procedure for the greatest companies in the world. If you are reinventing business and want to understand if your journey is following the path of other great ventures, look no farther than *Collaborative Disruption* for a view of a kindred spirit and a great tale of support and inspiration."

—John Green, principal, Green Insights Group

"Changing entrenched cultures and processes takes tremendous courage and tenacity. Tom Muccio became a master of it, and *Collaborative Disruption* provides an entertaining account of how the transformation happened with Walmart and P&G. I am still successfully reapplying the lessons learned within large companies, start-ups and non-profit organizations."

—Bill Toler, global vice president (retired), P&G

"Tom Muccio's new book is not a business book, rather, it is a history of two corporate giants, leery of change while concurrently realizing change is necessary for survival. The genius of the book is that it reads like a military after action report, detailing what happened, why it happened and how it can be replicated."

"*Collaborative Disruption* isn't just the Walmart-P&G story, it's the story of how to build a collaborative team. Our leader, Tom Muccio, was driven, but he used that drive to inspire us to our best and beyond. We'd show up at 5 A.M. some days, but we wanted to because Tom knew how to motivate with a positive focus and joy. Tom taught all of us that a great culture starts with people—choosing the right people, and then creating a space where they can be set free to do their best work."

"In my time on P&G's Walmart Team, I learned important lessons about multi-functional teamwork, leadership, and partnership across customer and supplier. These lessons benefited me for the rest of my career!"

"Tom describes the fantastic process of the design and implementation of the amazing transformation known as Customer Business Development. The time I spent working for Tom on the Walmart/P&G design team has made my career. It enabled me to contribute my ideas to the design and learn so many skills that have been in use ever since. I was able to take the concept to Europe and generate amazing relationships with many customers highlighted by the phenomenal success of our Tesco Global Team, which I led for many years. I still use all I learned in my many business interests since retiring from P&G."

"The journey of Walmart and Procter & Gamble is a testament to the enduring power of collaborative innovation. This book is not a collection of war stories and recollections, but a master class for any leader wanting to dramatically change the trajectory of their customer collaboration, culture, and performance."

—Rich Kley, head of sales, LatinUs Beauty; former sales director, Poland and the Baltic States, P&G

Collaborative Disruption

Collaborative Disruption

The Walmart and P&G Partnership
That Changed Retail Forever

Tom Muccio

Foreword by John Pepper

Fayetteville | 2024

Manufactured in the United States of America

978-1-954892-18-7 (cloth)
978-1-954892-20-0 (paperback)
978-1-954892-19-4 (e-book)

28 27 26 25 24 5 4 3 2 1

♾ The paper used in this publication meets the minimum requirements of the American National Standard for Permanence of Paper for Printed Library Materials Z39.48-1984.

Library of Congress Control Number: 2024934529

This book is dedicated to ...

The hundreds of Walmart associates and P&G team members who were the original pioneers and who put their career prospects on the line to bring this transformational, yet organizationally challenging idea to life. I wish I could have referenced every team member because each has a story worth telling. While every name may not be in the book, everyone's fingerprints are all over the results.

The handful of executives in both P&G and Walmart who sponsored the concept and provided the support to get it off the ground.

The thousands of people from the combined companies who have built on the foundation and who continue to build on this relationship. In particular, Jeff Schomburger and Mindy Sherwood, who followed me as the Global P&G Team Leaders and have built on and extended the relationship for more than twenty years.

The successive CEOs of both companies who have embraced, encouraged, and participated in the growth and impact of the relationship.

Contents

Foreword: A Revolution in Retailing   ix
Acknowledgments   xi

Introduction: An Atypical Biography   3

PART I: It Starts at the Top

1   Don't Unpack   13

2   Tie Your Loafers   19

3   Lou and the Canoe   27

4   Let's Do It . . . I'll Get Back to You   33

5   Intentional Design   39

6   Shooting Birds, Hitting Pringles   45

PART II: One Team, One Dream

7   Setting Up Shop   53

8   Building the Bike Path   63

9   Structural Integrity   73

10   Two in the Front   81

11   Comparative Cultures   91

12   The Path of the Pathfinders   101

13   Sharing the Story   115

PART III: Battling the Barriers

14 Walk toward the Barking Dog 125

15 Here Be Dragons 137

16 The Problem with Incentives 145

PART IV: Everybody Bring a Hammer

17 Learn Fast, Fix Fast, Scale Fast 155

18 Every Day Is the Big Game 163

19 Ski on Two Skis 169

PART V: A Promise Made Is a Promise Kept

20 The Payoff of Trust 175

21 Expanding the Model 179

22 The Triune Mandate 185

23 Seasons of Change 193

Epilogue: My Long Walk to Change 199

Appendix A: Vision of the Future 203

Appendix B: Mirror Team Members 207

Appendix C: Customer Team Mission, Vision, and Values 209

Appendix D: Tom Muccio's Personal Operating Philosophy and Expectations 211

Appendix E: Language Matters—A Glossary of Muccioisms 215

Index 221

Foreword

A Revolution in Retailing

I have observed and personally been part of many game-changing collaborations in the course of my career, but I can think of none that surpass the business growth from the partnership formed between the Procter & Gamble Company (P&G) and Walmart, starting in 1987 and continuing to today.

I believe it is fair to describe the Walmart-P&G partnership as launching a revolution in retailing. It changed the way suppliers and customers could work together at their best—as one company, pursuing mutual objectives, capitalizing on their combined talent.

The political philosopher Hannah Arendt once argued, "At its best, revolution demonstrates the human capacity for beginning genuinely new things through the creative action of individual human beings." I can think of no more succinct summation of what the Walmart-P&G partnership achieved in the retailing industry.

In *Collaborative Disruption*, Tom Muccio, the initial leader of the Walmart-P&G team, has written a granular, personal history of this revolutionary change. He describes how two entities that had been battling over a zero-sum playing field moved to one that demonstrated, by understanding and working together, results far beyond what was imagined, ultimately to the benefit of those whom both organizations served—consumers.

Tom's history of this partnership brings to life in a highly engaging way principles and values—keys to success—that I believe will be relevant today to organizational leaders seeking to build value and strategic relationships with a partner.

This history highlights the importance of continuity: the Walmart-P&G team has had only three leaders over its thirty-five-plus-year history. It highlights the importance of leadership from the top—the CEOs at P&G and Walmart supported and followed this relationship closely from day one to today. It highlights the importance of candor and openness, being willing to put the proverbial "moose on the table." Above all, it highlights the reality that progress depends on relationships and that relationships are founded on trust.

Very importantly, Tom shows how the "intent to build trust" must be mobilized by a framework of principles (candor and mutual respect) and operating practices and processes (including rigorous accountability) that allow the parties to build sustained trust.

I worked with Tom, other members of the P&G team, and many of the Walmart leaders for over fifteen years. I was always lifted by the qualities of the relationship within the P&G team and the relationship between the P&G and Walmart leaders: a refusal to accept the status quo; a willingness to establish stretch and breakthrough objectives and develop extraordinarily detailed plans to reach them; and honesty, candor, and mutual respect in the relationships among all the parties.

Above all, I experienced people committed to excellence and who cared deeply about the purpose of the organization, about the people it serves, and about each other.

John Pepper
Retired CEO, Procter & Gamble

Acknowledgments

I t is fitting that a book on collaborative disruption resulted from a collaborative process that, at times at least, was quite disruptive!

I thank my wife, Nancy; my daughter, Kirsty; and my son, Mike, for their unwavering support during my role as team leader. There were many disruptions in their lives (not always collaboratively) that allowed the results to be what they were.

Former team members worked with me on multiple attempts over the years to capture and record the unvarnished history of the background, beginning, and journey of the first fifteen years of the P&G-Walmart relationship. Each false start moved us forward until we gained traction in 2023. I am thankful for their encouragement not to give up on it and for their insights that shaped the story.

Andy Murray, a P&G member who went on to found what is now Saatchi & Saatchi X and subsequently was a senior officer at Walmart in the United States and in the United Kingdom, was a driving force behind the book, and his wonderful insights and fingerprints are all over it. It is no stretch to say this book would never have been published without him.

I am also thankful to the folks at the University of Arkansas's Sam M. Walton College of Business for agreeing to take on and publish this book. In particular, I am grateful for the support of Ryan Sheets, the publisher of the EPIC Books imprint; Stephen Caldwell, who helped wordsmith the manuscript with great sensitivity to the heart of each story; and Walton College dean Brent Williams.

Several former P&G team members consented to interviews or reviewed iterative versions of the manuscript, and each of them made it considerably better. Brian Barkocy, Don Bechtel, Harry Campbell, Jesse Edelman, Mike Graen, John Green, Henry Ho, Dina Howell, Rich Kley,

Andy Murray, Lou Pritchett, Bill Toler, and Tom Verdery all contributed with interviews.

Lou, my former boss and the instigator of the revolution that led P&G to disrupt the way it worked with customers like Walmart, also supported the project with his personal papers and by reviewing parts of the book. Former P&G CEO A. G. Lafley graciously responded to questions I sent him via email and encouraged me to complete the project, as did former CEO John Pepper, who also wrote the foreword.

I also want to acknowledge how fortunate I was to work with and learn from the top leaders within Walmart and P&G.

Sam Walton, of course, was one of the greatest leaders in the history of business, so I tried to absorb as much as possible from our time together. Perhaps the quality I admired most and tried to emulate as much as I could was his ability to be tough and demanding but at the same time incredibly caring. When he talked with people, Sam looked them in the eyes, called them by their names, and showed that he genuinely was interested in who they were beyond whatever position they held. Hopefully some of those attributes rubbed off on me along the way.

I also learned much from my frequent contacts with David Glass and particularly Don Soderquist, who was a "real time" mentor and friend.

Leaders at P&G like John Smale, Tom Laco, Lou Pritchett, Mike Milligan, Gerry Dirvin, John Pepper, and A. G. Lafley, meanwhile, modeled the type of courage I needed to emulate. I saw integrity and kindness in John Pepper. I saw perseverance in Lou Pritchett. I saw resourcefulness in Tom Laco. I saw encouragement with toughness and honesty in Mike Milligan. I saw the importance of behind-the-scenes influence from Gerry Dirvin. I saw the power of empowering others in A. G. Lafley. And I saw humility in John Smale.

I am also thankful for mentors from other areas of my life who shaped who I became as a leader. In particular, Ken Blanchard constantly reminded me that the sheep aren't there for the benefit of the shepherd. Just the opposite. Leaders end up getting more than their fair share of the credit just because that's the way the world looks at it. No matter how smart or how clever you think you are, you have to remember that any two people on your team will be better than you if you combine them, because the power of the team is incredible.

And importantly, I want to acknowledge My Lord and Savior Jesus Christ, who allowed me the opportunity to participate in both the team experience and the recording of it in this book. Time after time, when we needed direction, issue resolution, or favor, I went to Him in prayer and He never failed to help me.

Collaborative Disruption

Introduction

An Atypical Biography

If you enjoy biographies, then I suspect you will enjoy this book.

It's not typical of that genre, however, because it's not about a person. It's not even a typical corporate biography, because it's not about a company.

Instead, this is the biography of a relationship between two of the most successful companies on the planet—Walmart and Procter & Gamble (P&G)—and the transformative impact their collaborative disruption has had on business for more than thirty years, particularly in the retail industry.

It is a story worth telling for at least two significant reasons: it's great history, and it's relevant for today's business leaders.

Lessons from the Past

First, it's rare that anything happens in business that's truly a game-changer. This is the story of a game-changing initiative, so it holds historical significance.

It's easy and common, as Simon Sinek once pointed out, to confuse innovation with novelty. "Real innovation changes the course of industries or even society," Sinek wrote. "The light bulb, the microwave oven, the fax machine, iTunes. These are true innovations that changed how we conduct business."[1]

The collaborative relationship we came to call the "one-company model" isn't as well-known as iTunes, but it was game-changing to the industry because it fundamentally disrupted how suppliers and their retail customers interact with each other. These relationships almost universally are less transactional and more strategic, with suppliers emphasizing customer business development over traditional sales.

P&G had so much success with Walmart that we quickly rolled out the model with other customers around the globe. And while large retailers can have a deep and truly strategic alliance with only a handful of top suppliers, almost every supplier that sells products in Walmart or in other important retailers now uses at least some of the principles and best practices that emerged from the P&G-Walmart relationship.

In fact, by 2023 there were more than twelve hundred suppliers with offices in Northwest Arkansas to serve Walmart—up from one (P&G) when the first cross-functional teams from the two companies (collectively known as the mirror team) first met in 1989.

Some suppliers, despite their presence in the area, continue to have a transactional relationship with Walmart. Others have developed a value-added relationship. And a few, like P&G, have a truly strategic collaboration. None, however, approach Walmart or any other retail customer the way they did in the 1980s. None.

It was game-changing for Walmart and P&G because it played a significant role in their incredible growth. P&G already was an industry leader and a global player in the 1980s, but it needed to revitalize its model to remain competitive. Growing its business with Walmart—from 3.5 percent of its business to 16 percent of its business in less than twenty years—provided the shot P&G needed to capitalize on the rapidly changing retail landscape.

Don Bechtel, a supply chain expert and key P&G team member from the start, recalled a top-to-top meeting when the one-company idea was in its formative stages. We were doing about $350 million with Walmart at the time, and Walmart founder Sam Walton asked us how big we thought we could grow with this relationship. We told him we were shooting for $1 billion.

"I like the way you boys think," Sam told us.

He also liked the way we delivered, because we hit the $1 billion mark in three years. And from 1989 to 2003 (when I retired), P&G's business with Walmart went from $350 million a year to $8 billion a year. P&G's sales to Walmart alone would have ranked it at number 234 on the *Fortune* 500 list.

Walmart, meanwhile, was mainly a regional retailer in the 1980s. When the collaboration began, Walmart was an up-and-coming retailer, but it was just starting to experiment with Supercenters and had no stores outside the United States. It also was losing money (about 4 percent annually) on its combined sales of P&G products, which mainly served as loss leaders to draw in shoppers who also purchased more products with positive profit margins.

No one would suggest Walmart would not have become the world's biggest company without the P&G collaboration, but it clearly was a positive part of that story. And it didn't take long for us to solve the issues that caused Walmart to lose money on our products. By the early 1990s Walmart had a 2 percent profit margin on P&G brands, and that grew to 8 percent by the end of the decade and double digits in the early 2000s.

Lessons for Today

The second significant reason this story is worth telling is that it, like any good biography, conveys some important lessons leaders can apply to modern collaborations and business partnerships.

There may be a tendency for some to dismiss a book about events that mostly took place twenty-five to thirty years ago.

"Thank you, Grandpa, for sharing what it was like in the good old days, but what's all that have to do with me?" those skeptics would say. "Things have changed so much since you retired that any lessons you can share either aren't relevant or are already in place as table stakes."

I not only disagree, but I take exception to both of these heresies! Courage, innovation, and people development never go out of style.

The processes we used and the lessons we learned are highly relevant to any leaders involved in creating a collaborative partnership between two companies, engaging in change management, or creating cross-functional internal teams that work well together with other parts of their internal organization.

There's hardly a company of any size that isn't involved in at least one of those high-stakes initiatives in today's fast-paced, volatile economic environment. And collaborative efforts between industry, universities, governments, and nonprofits have become critical to economic growth and development.

Collaborative Disruption tells the behind-the-scenes story of how these two companies worked together to redefine the strategic operational relationship with each other and, ultimately, between all retailers and suppliers. And the model intentionally designed by that original team and improved over the years by a succession of talented leaders has become the gold standard for joint business partnerships.

While a great deal has changed in the marketplace and with the model itself, the values and principles behind how it was created, executed, and refined are as relevant as ever. Woven throughout the fabric of everything we did, for instance, were values like integrity and respect that shaped our thinking and our decisions.

This story illustrates those values and many of the traits every successful team needs, but particularly a multifunctional team that's collaborating with a business partner. As you read about our team, you will learn the following:

We had a vision. We really did see that there was a better way for the two companies to operate together. And we appreciated that visions need to be not only caught but also continually shared. So wherever we were or wherever we could, we talked about the possibilities that existed for a better way to work together.

We believed. We saw the amazing resources that existed within P&G and Walmart and the incredible people in both companies, so we had confidence that we could make a new reality.

We had passion. We were all willing to go the extra mile. If that meant working late into the night or working all weekend, we would willingly do whatever was required. Everybody had each other's back, and there was nothing you could ask someone to do that they weren't willing to do.

We had courage. There were many times that individuals had to put their career or reputation on the line to move us forward. We supported each other in those times, as well, so no one was walking the plank alone. But you still needed to have courage to take risks if you were going to make change happen.

We were persistent. Things often didn't work as planned, and we were told "no" many times within P&G and from Walmart. But if we believed it was the right thing to do, we found a way to get it done. We had a "never give up" mentality.

We were humble. The team realized that none of us were as strong or as good individually as we were collectively. When it came to taking credit, everyone was quick to defer to others. Pride, ego, and entitlement were the enemies of our success.

One of the ways I personally learned this was by watching Walmart's senior and middle management operate on a day-to-day basis, because they did not act as if they were entitled to anything other than the opportunity to contribute. They did their jobs with great passion and skill, and they didn't have reserved parking spots for executives or special rules that applied just for the leadership team.

We were grateful. Rather than harboring a sense of entitlement, the team was thankful for the experiences we were having together. It was amazing that we could be part of such a historic partnership and experience such incredible business and personal growth.

The applicable lessons around teamwork, strategies, and tactics make this far more than just a fascinating business case study—although it is that. Don't expect me to hand you a detailed playbook with proprietary models from the two companies. But I will offer plenty of transferable ideas and practices to any leader who values collaboration, whether it's among internal teams, in limited but important business-to-business partnerships, or in high-level strategic alliances.

The Real Story

As the first leader of the P&G team, it was my good fortune to have an insider's view of this partnership, from its genesis to its design to the first fifteen years of its success.

I'll tell the story from my perspective and in my own unique way. (You might run into a few "Muccioisms" along the way, and if you need definitions, they are in appendix E.) This account is based on my experiences, the notes I saved from my time as team leader, and the interviews I did with former team members who represent the hundreds of people from both companies who came together to make this miracle happen. But it's most certainly not a story about me.

It's really their story. And their story is one that lives on, because the one-company model proved to be a wonderful training ground for leaders who have gone on to do some amazing things in business, some with Walmart or P&G and others with other companies.

All of the original mirror team members from Walmart advanced at least to the level of vice president within their company. During my time as team leader at P&G, nine members of our team rose at least to vice president (Bill Toler, Tom O'Brien, Kim Robinson, Barron Witherspoon, Dina Howell, John Molter, Andy Jett, Jeff Schomburger, and me), including two who became presidents within the company (Schomburger and me). After my time, Mindy Sherwood and Eric Breissinger also became presidents, with Mindy eventually being named chief sales officer.

Many others who worked together and gained experience on the team went from P&G and Walmart to start new companies or lead other major companies—people like Jesse Edelman (CEO and founder, ArchPoint Group), Henry Ho (cofounder, NorthStar Partnering Group and Field Agent), Bill Waitsman (cofounder, NorthStar Partnering Group; CEO and founder, Harvest Group and One Stone), Tregg Brown (president, Team Direct), Brian Barren (president of business operations of the Cleveland Guardians), Kim Robinson (CEO, National Underground Railroad) and Andy Murray (cofounder and CEO of Saatchi & Saatchi X).

There are as many similar results from the Walmart side of the working relationship, including Bill Fields (CEO of Blockbuster and Hudson Bay Co.), Robert Bruce (founder and CEO of VCC Associates Inc.), Roger Gildehaus (founder and CEO of Macadoodles), Bobby Martin (president and CEO of Gap), and Joe Hardin Jr. (CEO of Kinko's).

The more I worked on this book, the more I found myself pinching my cheek and saying to myself, "I can't believe I was a part of it!"

We only accomplished something of this magnitude against all the odds we faced because hundreds of dedicated and talented people worked together like the world's greatest orchestra. Yes, I played a leadership role, but I was like a conductor who didn't read music and couldn't play any instruments. I waved a little baton and a bunch of gifted musicians played incredible music. Then, I was the first to stand and applaud.

The credit for the success of the Walmart and P&G collaboration goes first to the courageous leadership at the top of both companies who allowed the experiment to happen and then to the tireless, creative, and risk-taking people who brought it to life. And, most importantly from my viewpoint, it goes to the Lord, who lit the path, gave us favor, opened blind eyes, and occasionally made seeing eyes blind.

I hope you will join me on this deeply personal journey of a monumental success story that transformed the way companies can work together and that changed thousands of lives for the better—starting with mine.

Note

1. Simon Sinek, *Start with Why* (New York: Penguin, 2011), 26.

PART I

It Starts at the Top

All big transformations involving two different organizations require a commitment from the top. The Walmart partnership with P&G owes its origins to leaders at the top of each company who were willing to bet on and invest in a new way of doing business.

CHAPTER 1

Don't Unpack

There was something distinctly different about the second meeting of the mirror team—the small group of Walmart and P&G leaders who were tasked with figuring out the details of an unprecedented collaboration between the two companies.

The first meeting had gone smoothly enough, but on that day we were mostly picking low-hanging fruit.

The mirror team—around sixteen of us—consisted of peers from each company who "mirrored" each other's functional responsibilities (see the detailed list of the team in appendix B). This was the first time some of us had been in the same room at the same time, so part of our time was spent just getting to know each other. But we also reviewed the progress that had led us to that point, drafted a mission statement, and identified the work that needed to happen before we met again in four weeks. We left with a positive vibe hanging in the air.

When we reconvened on August 22, 1989, however, the magnitude of what we were trying to do—the realities of scope, the speed, and the complexity of this grand idea—came out of the clouds like a pop-up thunderstorm and landed squarely in our conference room in Fayetteville, Arkansas.

We needed a grand vision, and we had it. We needed a clear mission, and we had it. We needed good intentions, and we had them. But we were attempting something that had never been done—a totally new approach to a large-scale business partnership where employees from both companies would have access to internal workings of the other company. And to add to the challenge, this wasn't exactly a match made in heaven. More like a shotgun wedding, at least in the eyes of some.

By the mid-1980s, P&G had over a century of success under its belt and had grown into a global consumer products company. But we had a reputation as a bit of a bully when dealing with retailers who, in our collective corporate minds, couldn't survive without our high-quality brands.

Walmart, meanwhile, was an up-and-coming retailer that began with a store in the hills of Arkansas and had expanded across rural America at the speed of light. It won by focusing on operational efficiencies and "everyday low prices" instead of relying on discounting or promotional pricing.

And while Walmart sold most of P&G's products and each played a role in the other's success, the companies hardly knew each other. Their relationship, like the relationship between most suppliers and retailers at that time, was often fragmented, at times adversarial, and at best transactional.

None of that sat well with Lou Pritchett, who had taken the role of vice president of sales at P&G in 1985, or with Walmart's energetic and visionary founder, Sam Walton. But that's the way it was.

"Both [companies] focused on the end-user—the customer—but each did it independently of the other," Lou would say. "No sharing of information, no planning together, no systems coordination. We were simply two giant entities going our separate ways, oblivious to the excess costs created by this obsolete system. We were communicating, in effect, by slipping notes under the door."[1]

Sam put it even more succinctly: "We just let our buyers slug it out with their salesmen," he said, "and both sides lived with the results."[2]

In the summer of 1987, however, Sam and Lou met for the first time, and their conversation provided the spark that ignited transformation.

What if the two companies opened their hoods and let the other see inside? What if senior-level leaders shared relevant information—including proprietary information—in ways that helped both companies, not to mention consumers? What if they coordinated on things like supply chain systems, payment processes, information technology, and marketing? What if leaders at all levels put themselves in the shoes of their counterparts at the other company when making decisions?

To paraphrase Sam Walton, *what if they acted as one company?*

P&G and Walmart decided to put those "what ifs" to the test.

After a series of events that took less than two years, the top executives—Walton for Walmart and P&G CEO John Smale—went from being strangers who had never had so much as a phone conversation to becoming allies who endorsed the idea of forging a unique operating relationship between the behemoth retailer and the gargantuan supplier.

Simple enough, right?

In reality, of course, the test turned out to be pretty difficult—less of an open-book, check-the-boxes exam and more like the Spartan Death Race.

The Spartan Death Race is a mentally and physically grueling event in the rugged mountains of Vermont that can take up to seventy hours to produce a winner. Here's how the organizers bill it: "We provide no support. We don't tell you when it starts. We don't tell you when it ends. We don't tell you what it will entail. We want you to fail and encourage you to quit at any time."[3]

Who signs up for that?

Well, I guess the mirror team did!

While the all-important leaders at the highest levels were aligned on the big-picture idea, plenty of skeptics still roamed the hallways of both companies.

There was active opposition from those who resisted change. Some were winning with the existing system and didn't want to give up power even if it was better for their company and its customers. Others were unable to break free of existing bureaucracies that took the form of unyielding policies and procedures, many of them decades old. And, of course, there were mountains of differences in the mindsets, operating approaches, and cultures of P&G and Walmart.

As the leader of an internal P&G team that already had been exploring new ways of going to market, I was put in charge of the group that would work directly with Walmart. In only a year, we had conducted initial research, developed ideas about what we wanted to achieve, tested a few projects, and even opened an office in Fayetteville, Arkansas, about forty miles from Walmart's headquarters in Bentonville.

A few members of the cross-functional P&G team we were creating had already bought homes in this strange new world. Others, like me, were commuting between Arkansas and the P&G home office in Cincinnati, but we were making plans to sell our homes. Two years earlier most of us couldn't find Arkansas on a map. Now we were packing up to move there.

All that remained was to figure out how to make this bold, new strategic partnership actually work on a day-in-and-day-out basis. And we had to figure it out quickly, because the year we'd been given to test and plan was nearing its end.

Broadly speaking, that was the goal for the mirror team in 1989 when we gathered for just the second time: figure out the nitty-gritty details of how to make this work—and fast!

Finance, information technology, supply chain, analytics, store operations, marketing, human resources, and sales/buying were among the functions initially represented by each company on the mirror team, but now we were all part of one team, at least theoretically.

We all knew, however, that the two companies were as different as night and day. At P&G, we were very much into business processes, for instance, while the Walmart culture was more practical and action oriented. And while we shared some important values, P&G was signing our checks and Walmart paid our new friends. There was no way around that. So while we all came to day one of a two-day meeting with an intent to trust, we weren't yet sure what type of road we might pave with those good intentions, much less where it would lead.

For the experiment to work, the mirror team somehow had to align our shared focus areas and operating principles. If we couldn't do that, there wouldn't be much hope of moving forward.

Al Lennon, an organizational effectiveness leader for P&G, facilitated an exercise to get us started. Each team member had a stack of yellow sticky notes, and everyone wrote down what they saw as the opportunities and roadblocks of our fledgling partnership. Then we all took our sticky notes to the front of the room and put the opportunities on one flipchart and the roadblocks on another.

I'll never forget those two flipcharts. The one for opportunities held about five lonely stickies, while the one for roadblocks was plastered in so much yellow I thought we were in a banana farm—around two hundred notes!

It was the Walmart-P&G version of the Spartan Death Race, and the odds of our survival weren't looking too good.

When I called home to Cincinnati that night, my wife greeted me with her typical good cheer and asked me how the day went.

Not good, I told her.

"Honey," I said, "when we move here, don't be quick to unpack, it might be a short assignment."

Notes

1. Sam Walton, *Sam Walton: Made in America* (New York: Random House, 2012), Kindle edition, 238.
2. Walton, *Sam Walton: Made in America,* 237.
3. "Spartan Death Race," Peak Races, accessed April 15, 2024, https://peakraces.com/death-races/.

CHAPTER 2

Tie Your Loafers

N ancy and I unpacked our bags in Arkansas in 1990 and we never left. We changed addresses a few more times, but the P&G collaboration with Walmart became a monumental success story, and Arkansas became our adopted home.

Day two of the mirror team's second meeting in 1989 went much better than day one, and progress continued. Before long, Walmart and P&G redefined their strategic operational relationship with each other and, ultimately, between all retailers and suppliers.

Our original cross-functional team designed what became known as the one-company operating model. The model still isn't widely known or practiced to the degree we implemented it, but imitation—even partial imitation—remains the sincerest form of flattery. And as we had success with the partnerships, others did their best to replicate what they saw happening. We used to joke that if we hired a dog catcher on our P&G team, our competitors would hire one, too, and they'd never ask why.

As a result, almost every supplier that sells products in Walmart now uses at least some of the principles and best practices that emerged from the P&G relationship, although none, to my knowledge, employ dog catchers.

In retrospect, you might wonder why such a collaboration hadn't happened earlier. Or, once it was started, you might think it was destined to succeed. You might even see it as the somewhat organic result of evolving business relationships.

Such conclusions are understandable, but off base. Remember: Objects in mirrors can be closer than they appear. The way it is now is not the way it was back then. And the way it was back then might seem hard to imagine now.

To get a feel for the challenges the mirror team faced, it's helpful to revisit the 1980s, an era when mall food courts were newly in vogue, music videos were the hottest thing on television, every child wanted a Cabbage Patch Kid, and a mostly regional retail chain called Wal-Mart (it still used a hyphen in its name) was experimenting with formats it called "hypermarts" and "supercenters."

In 1987, when the first seeds of the partnership were planted, Walmart had fewer than two thousand stores (all in the United States) and two hundred thousand associates. It rang up $15.9 billion in sales, which was impressive at the time but nowhere near what it is today—the world's largest company, with more than ten thousand stores in twenty countries, more than 2.1 million associates, and roughly $570 billion in annual sales.

Back then, Walmart catered mainly to rural and suburban markets. And while it was an important customer for P&G, our biggest US customers were Kmart and Kroger. Walmart was fourth on that list, also behind SuperValu but ahead of the drugstores and supermarkets known as American Stores.

P&G, meanwhile, was founded in 1837, 125 years before Walmart. We already were a global enterprise and a juggernaut in the consumer goods industry. There was a lot of "great" in that history, but times were changing, and we were about to find out if we could lead the change or if we would become prisoners of our past.

In the 1980s, P&G had eight product divisions—packaged soap and detergents (known as "big soap"), bar soap and household cleaning products ("little soap"), food, beverage, paper, health care, beauty care, and food service and lodging. Each had its own management group and its own sales force. The vice presidents of the product divisions, not the vice president of sales, controlled things like salary increases, stock options, and promotions, and they were extremely protective of their decision-making power.

The sales teams in the eight divisions were organized by geography, not by major retailers. They all called on Walmart (and other retailers) independently of each other, often with different terms and requirements. There was little sharing across those divisions about opportunities, issues, or procedures, and even less sharing with the retailer customers.

As one of my colleagues would later say, it was like P&G had taken a Mercedes and broken it into eight bicycles. But the one thing the sales teams had in common was that they tended to operate from a position of power over the retailers who bought our products and sold them to consumers.

This was typical of all supplier-retailer relationships at the time. As Sam Walton would later note, "I don't mind saying that we were the victims of a good bit of arrogance from a lot of vendors in those days. They didn't need us, and they acted that way."[1]

This was destined to change.

I was national sales manager for P&G's food division in 1985 when Lou Pritchett returned from an assignment in the Philippines to become vice president of global sales. Lou likes to say he came back and rocked the boat. The way I see it, he lit the fuse that blew up the way we went to market.

Lou already had been thinking about the value of business partnerships. In fact, at the 1982 annual meeting of the Philippine Association of Supermarkets, Lou delivered a keynote address that challenged suppliers to work more collaboratively with P&G.

"That was the first time I'd ever mentioned the word *partnering*," Lou told me.[2]

In that speech, Lou laid out eleven points on how the manufacturers in the Philippines could partner with P&G to improve their overall business.

"Rather than simply trying to sell me bigger orders," Lou later wrote, "I would insist that they bring to me solid ideas which, when implemented, would automatically result in large orders. I would strongly advocate for a *partnership* between us."[3]

Since Lou had been living and working overseas for four years, he naturally wanted to get up to speed on everything related to our work and our customers. And he wanted to start practicing what he'd been preaching in the Philippines.

"When I came back from the Philippines, I was even more convinced that we needed to do more work with customers—understanding them and sharing," he told me. "So that's when I started looking around for our big customers. Walmart was not nearly as big as Kmart, so I went to see Joe Antonini."[4]

The meeting with Antonini, then the CEO of Kmart, didn't take long.

As Lou recalled it, Antonini said, "Mr. Pritchett, let me be real honest with you. I'd rather deal with a thread salesman than a [blankety-blank] soap salesman."[5] In other words, America's second-largest retailer (behind Sears) cared more about selling clothing than P&G's products.

Undeterred, Lou looked at other retailers and discovered that Walmart was one of our larger customers but also one with whom we had the most problems. So one day he met with the eight national sales managers and asked us a pretty simple question: "Can one of you fill me in on this customer?"

Collectively, it was if we all bent over to tie our loafers under the table so we could avoid eye contact with Lou. Since we managed our businesses by geography not by customer, we could tell him about the business in Los Angeles, Atlanta, Boston, or Dallas, but not Walmart. They operated mostly in small towns in the south and their headquarters was in Bentonville, Arkansas, so they weren't on anyone's radar.

"I'll do my own research," Lou told us. "And when I find out about this customer, I'll advise you gentlemen, as well."

Our lack of a good answer to Pritchett's question also spurred him to launch two teams that had special assignments. One was the Jacksonville (Florida) Test Team led by Wayne Galloway, which tested a model that reduced our sales force calling on retail stores to just two—one for health and beauty aids and the other for the rest of the product divisions. The other was a multifunctional design team that was charged with researching and recommending changes to our "go to market" strategy.

That team, which I led, included highly competent people from different functions within P&G who had one thing in common: like Lou, we weren't afraid to speak out. This resulted in a relatively rebellious group that wasn't particularly popular within P&G, which at the time was a company where the status quo in organization structure was almost deified.

Lou and this team were challenging the existing system. Several of the product sales managers felt conflicted and sought protection from Lou with their product division vice presidents. This quickly put a target on Lou, an outgoing and vocal visionary who became known as a "rabble rouser" in the eyes of those other vice presidents. And the sales managers like me who aligned with Lou also were seen as threats by our other colleagues and their bosses.

So my new team and I jumped in with Lou and helped him rock P&G's boat.

We looked at every function in the company and highlighted strengths, negatives, and outages (things that are missing that shouldn't be missing). We did deep-dive research on our competitors and on industry leaders in a variety of companies. We hired outside futurists to get their views on how each function would evolve. And we looked at all of our customers, including Walmart.

In fact, we even did a focus group that included representatives from Walmart and P&G talking about their pain points in working with each other. Whenever someone argued that everything was just fine the way it was, all we had to do was point to a video we had made of that focus group. As coaches like to tell their players, the film doesn't lie.

An expert in change management encouraged us to create an executive team that included senior functional managers and product general managers so we could process what we learned in real time and, in theory, garner support as the process proceeded. This executive steering team met with our design team every two weeks for an update on what we had learned.

Fortunately, John Pepper led the steering team. John was president of P&G's US business and eventually would serve as the company's CEO. He was a great leader, a fast learner, and a good listener, and his presence ensured attendance from the rest of the team.

Interestingly, A. G. Lafley was on that steering team, and he later became P&G's CEO (from 2000 to 2010 and from 2013 to 2015).

"Many of my best memories of thirty-six-plus years at P&G involve Walmart," A. G. told me in an email not long ago. "I don't know how my name got pulled out of the hat, but I do remember being the only advertising/marketing person and the most junior player on the small team you pulled together to do early planning for the partnership."[6]

As CEO, A. G. codified the importance of the customer to P&G's strategy and made significant changes that gave legs to his words. For instance, he identified P&G's two "moments of truth" with consumers—one in the store when they were deciding what to buy and the other when they used the product. And he created three types of general managers at the same level—product, customer, and geography—and designed a process that required collaboration among the three. This elevated customer work to the strategic level in the company.

In those early years, however, leaders like John Pepper were guiding our ship. And later on, when the decision was made to proceed with the

Walmart team test and move to Northwest Arkansas, John ensured we had adequate resources to get started, additional resources along the way, assistance with accountability, and aligned expectations.

Throughout my time leading the team, Walmart's senior leadership held John in the highest regard. Doug Degn, a former executive vice president at Walmart, for instance, described one meeting he had in Cincinnati with John as "life changing" both professionally and personally. John had shared a video, "The Smell of the Place" featuring management professor Sumantra Ghoshal, that contrasted summers in Calcutta with springs in Fontainebleau, France. They then discussed how that comparison plays out in the way executives' actions influence their cultures.

John even served as a consultant to Sam and Rob Walton as they considered and initiated their entry into China. And as the team leader, I always felt he had my back and would provide an open door to process internal alignment issues and resourcing.

When it came to our internal design team's work, John and the steering team weren't the final decision makers, but their involvement kept the process from being just the design team alone and it helped make the recommendations much clearer, sharper, and better supported.

At each meeting with the steering team, we'd share what we had learned and how we felt it fit into the overall objective of an improved way of going to market with our customers. They often disagreed with our conclusions and at times they wanted more information, which we'd get. But once we reached an agreement in an area, we would put a proverbial stake in the ground so we could move on to something else.

Several realities emerged that would shape our final recommendations.

The biggest thing we realized was that retailers didn't understand anything about how consumer product manufacturers like P&G operated, and P&G didn't have a very good understanding of how retailers worked.

Retailers, for instance, had no concept of the amount of research and development or customer research that went into products. And while we were experts on our brands and our categories, we didn't really know how our product went through a retail customer's system and the issues they had.

Most of our emphasis was on the internal issues we could address to improve P&G's working relationship with retail customers. For instance,

- While companies like Merrill Lynch provided daily updated stock portfolio details to their clients, it took P&G three weeks after a month ended to get reports on our shipments for a customer. And we had no system that combined all the P&G product divisions' shipments with any one customer.
- We reviewed our business with our customers based on our fiscal quarters and fiscal year rather than theirs.
- Our customers managed their businesses in sales dollars, while we reviewed our business with them using an internal measurement called "stat cases." Do you know what a stat case is? Neither did anyone at Walmart or any other retailer. A statistical case, or stat case, was our way of equating products as diverse as a big box of detergent and a small box with tubes of toothpaste.
- Our information technology with customers was a major outage (it didn't exist).
- While all companies coordinate their functions toward achieving their primary goal, our interactions with retail customers were tactical and transactional. It only involved sales, accounts payable, and warehouse receiving, ignoring all the other functions that it takes to run a business.

It was during this period that we also recognized the very real frustration and confusion our customers felt as a result of how independently our eight product divisions operated. Those divisions had different policies and payment terms, for instance, but all of their invoices said Procter & Gamble.

The most important conclusions by our team were that we needed to go to market with our customers as a multifunctional group, and we needed more consistency in the way our product divisions interacted within P&G and with our external retail customers.

We recommended making improvements to the internal and external information systems P&G used to do business with our customers, and better communication and collaboration on strategies designed to meet the objectives of both the product divisions and the category managers within each of those divisions.

Our most radical recommendation, however, was to "colocate" the teams working with retail customers so that we had people from multifunctions in the same location as our customers' headquarters. That, we argued, would substantially improve access and communication and allow for more meaningful business relationships to form and prosper.

Another outcome of our work was a "vision of the future" document (see appendix A) specific to our relationship with Walmart, which I'm sure we did because of Lou's interest in that particular customer. It was written in February 1987 but as if we were looking back on a successful five years while living in the year 1992. So it was forecasting how we saw the relationship five years into the future.

Frankly, we were amazingly accurate.

We described a "cooperative effort" between Walmart and P&G that had led to "significantly increased market shares for both companies." The collaboration, we predicted, was a "highly effective and efficient business-building partnership based on common long-term objectives and mutual trust." Then we laid out nine characteristics of the business relationship.

Our conclusions, recommendations, and vision statement were not well received by the product divisions or most of the functions at P&G. Selling that type of change would be an uphill battle, and the hill looked like the White Cliffs of Dover. Debates took place in all corners of the company, and our design team realized that there wasn't enough traction anywhere within P&G to get us out of the starting gate.

What we didn't know at the time was that our internal design team wasn't alone in making waves. Lou Pritchett and Sam Walton were stirring up the waters as well, and their float trip on the Spring River would change the course of history for all of us.

Notes

1. Sam Walton, *Sam Walton: Made in America* (New York: Random House, 2012), Kindle edition, 66.
2. Lou Pritchett, interview with the author, 2023.
3. Lou Pritchett, *What the Internet Can't Teach You* (Bloomington, IN: iUniversity, 2011), 117.
4. Pritchett, interview.
5. Pritchett, interview.
6. A. G. Lafley, email interview with the author, 2023.

CHAPTER 3

Lou and the Canoe

I think back on our first canoe trip and how we evolved our partnership process with Procter & Gamble. It was one of the best things that ever happened to our company and I think time bears out that many other companies are beginning to view the supplier as an important partner.

—Sam Walton to Lou Pritchett, January 16, 1991

Many of us familiar with the history of Walmart's partnership with P&G have assumed that Sam Walton and Lou Pritchett first discussed the state of the relationship between the two companies in 1987 while floating down the Spring River together in a canoe, taking a lunch break on a sandbar, or sitting around a campfire at night.

In reality, the room where it happened was a school bus.

The famous canoe story is central to how everything came together, so it's important to share it for those who don't know it and worth repeating it with more details for those who think they know it. To go beyond the oral traditions or the versions that are in books, articles, and a few cases studies, I gave Lou a call to confirm what I thought was true and see if he might add more details.

As always, Lou didn't disappoint me.

So, based on Sam's book, Lou's three books, and my emails and phone calls with Lou, I think I can offer the most complete version of this story that's ever been told.

One of the ways Lou kept his promise to learn more about Walmart was by reaching out to one of his old friends, George Billingsley. Lou and George both grew up in Memphis and first met in 1949 when they worked together at Kamp Kia Kima, a Boy Scout camp on the banks of the South Fork of the Spring River in northeast Arkansas. The camp had been closed during World War II, and George, Lou, and six other teens from Memphis helped reopen it.

George graduated from the University of Arkansas and Lou went to Memphis State College (now the University of Memphis), and they each had stints in the military. Then George settled down near the UA and Lou began his career at P&G. But their group had become close friends while spending their summers on staff at the camp, and the eight of them regularly came back to the area for reunions.

"It dawned on me after I worked with one of our salesmen in Arkansas that this account up in Northwest Arkansas was growing like crazy," Lou told me. "That's when I called George and said, 'Do you know this guy Walton?'"[1]

Indeed he did. George and Sam were friends and frequently played tennis together. So Lou asked if George could arrange for him to meet with the Walmart founder.

You don't want to have a meeting with him in his office, Billingsley told Pritchett. *He's not an office-type guy. He spends most of his time in his stores.*

Then George, who at the time owned a travel company that mostly catered to wealthy clients, suggested they invite Sam to join them for their next reunion on the Spring River. George and his wife had gone on float trips on the Buffalo River with Sam and Helen Walton, and he figured they would enjoy this type of adventure. Lou agreed, and George brought up the idea with Sam.

"So I went along," Sam would later say, "and it turned out to be the most productive float trip I ever took with George."[2]

Sam, for his part, was eager to have a discussion with someone—anyone—from P&G. In 1985, about the time Lou was returning from the Philippines, Sam was in the habit of punishing his buyers by assigning them to work with P&G's salespeople. But like Lou, he believed a healthier relationship would be better for both companies. So in an attempt to connect with P&G's top leaders and get a conversation started, Sam selected P&G for Walmart's prestigious "Vendor of the Year Award."

Sam called P&G CEO John Smale to inform him of the decision and invite John to Arkansas to receive the award. Back then, however, all calls from P&G's customers were routed to the sales teams, so Sam's call was redirected—and redirected and redirected. No one really knew who should take a call from a customer's founder. And after talking to multiple administrative assistants, a frustrated Walton gave up and gave the award to a different supplier.

Now, just a few years later, someone from P&G was calling on him—and he wanted to meet on a river, of all places.

The Spring River, which flows through parts of Missouri and into Arkansas, offers excellent fishing and long stretches where you can canoe, kayak, or just float along on an inflated tube. The cool, spring-fed waters are generally calm but can rise to Class III rapids in a few places along the South Fork of the river.

Most of the outfitters operate near Hardy, Arkansas, a town with fewer than a thousand residents that's a little more than a two-hour drive from Memphis. That's where the group agreed to meet—Lou and Barbara Pritchett, Sam and Helen Walton, George and Boyce Billingsley, and the others who had worked on staff with George and Lou at Kamp Kia Kima.

Sam, a pilot, was scheduled to fly in on his personal plane, while Lou and Barbara took the P&G corporate airplane. When they reached Hardy, however, they discovered the P&G plane was too big to land at that airport, and they had to land about forty curvy miles away in Walnut Ridge, Arkansas. Still, they made it to the rendezvous point by 5 p.m., an hour ahead of time, and waited.

And waited.

And waited.

"When the clock hit 7, I almost panicked," Lou told me. "I said I'll get fired bigger than hell when I get back to the office for taking this multi-million-dollar airplane to Walnut Ridge, Arkansas, to meet a customer who was a non-show. About that time, Sam walked in."[3]

The groups stayed in nearby Cherokee Village, a community founded in 1954 by George's father-in-law, but it wasn't long before Lou experienced a classic encounter with Sam.

"The next day, Sam borrowed a dollar from me to buy a banana split," Lou recalled. "He said, 'I left my billfold because I didn't want to wear it in my swim trunks. Do you happen to have any money on you?' So I gave him a dollar."[4]

Later when I got to know Sam and regularly did store checks with him, he sometimes would hit me up for money to buy his lunch, usually just a bowl of soup. I would buy his lunch, and he'd tell me to drop by his office to get reimbursed. After about the third time that happened, I said, "Sam, I now know why you are the richest man in the world. You don't pay for anything!"

Sam not only was thrifty with money, but he was also a master listener with a razor-sharp memory and a unique ability to spot great ideas and motivate the people around him. So now that he had an audience with a P&G vice president, he was eager to listen, learn, and explore new ideas with Lou, who was equally eager to do the same.

"As far as I am concerned," Lou said, "the whole purpose of the trip was for me to get to know Sam and Sam to get to know me."[5]

Sam was thirteen years older than Lou, but they both were Eagle Scouts who had served in the US Army, so they had plenty to talk about during casual conversations. While they were on the water, however, there weren't many opportunities to talk for long stretches. So when the outfitter directed the group to a school bus that would take them to their next launch spot in the river, Sam and Lou took a seat next to each other in the back.

Talk about getting the right people on the bus! There they talked until Lou's wife finally banged on the window and told them they were about to be left behind.

"The best discussions were when we moved from Point A to Point B, like when we moved from the South Fork to the Spring River," Lou said. "It was a long way with a lot of rapids and the water was low, so we went by school bus and Sam and I sat in the back, fourteen inches apart. That's where the real discussion began."[6]

Sam bemoaned the state of the Walmart relationship with P&G and made an observation that eventually became the rallying cry of both companies' teams: *If you thought of my stores as an extension of your company, we would be doing business entirely differently than today.*

Sam and Lou got off the school bus and back on the river, but they had taken the important first step toward change—they had agreed to make it happen.

The question was, who else would come along for the ride?

Notes

1. Lou Pritchett, interview with the author, 2023.
2. Sam Walton, *Sam Walton: Made in America* (New York: Random House, 2012), Kindle edition, 237.
3. Pritchett, interview.
4. Pritchett, interview.
5. Pritchett, interview.
6. Pritchett, interview.

CHAPTER 4

Let's Do It . . . I'll Get
Back to You

On October 9, 1987, just a few months after the canoe trip, Lou Pritchett and John Pepper visited Walmart's headquarters in Bentonville, Arkansas, where they met with Sam Walton and David Glass, who would serve as CEO from 1988 to 2000 but at the time was Walmart's president and COO.

They didn't leave with any type of formal agreement or plan, but Lou soon arranged for Sam and David to make a trip to Cincinnati for their first meeting with P&G CEO John Smale.

Lou and John Pepper, having visited the nondescript home offices of Walmart that David Glass referred to as having early bus station decor, already had a sense of the differences in the two companies' cultures. Now the P&G home team would get a taste of Walmart's atypical founder and his approach to life and business.

One Procter & Gamble Plaza in downtown Cincinnati provides nearly eight hundred thousand square feet of mostly office space, with two towers and two wings that stretch a full city block. The executive suites are known throughout the organization as the "11th Floor," so that's where Lou took Sam and David for their first meeting with John Smale.

One of the more interesting accounts of this meeting came from a food service employee who served the executives their morning coffee. When the waitress poured Sam's coffee into the fine china common throughout the 11th Floor, he asked John if all P&G employees drank their coffee in fine china cups. So John put the question to the waitress.

"The employees drink coffee served from coffee carts that we roll throughout the buildings," she said. "The coffee is served in Styrofoam cups."

"Then I'll have mine in a Styrofoam cup," Sam said.

Word also soon spread from the P&G travel department that Sam had turned down their reservation for him to stay at the Omni Hotel and chose a budget motel instead.

Lou didn't recall the coffee cup conversation, but he did remember something else Sam observed that day: "Now I know who makes all the money selling soap!"[1]

At the end of that first day, Lou took Sam and David to the Montgomery Inn, a well-known eatery in a suburb of Cincinnati known locally as "the ribs king." But Sam left early to fly his own plane through a rainstorm because he had a breeding appointment in St. Louis for his bird dogs. Lou tried to convince him to stay, enjoy the meal, and leave when the weather improved, but Sam made his priorities clear.

"When breeding dogs," he told Lou, "timing is everything."[2]

It wouldn't take long before Sam would return, because the timing also was right for P&G and Walmart to move their relationship into uncharted waters.

Around this time, Total Quality Management (TQ) was sweeping through the consumer products industry as a means of detecting and reducing errors while creating greater efficiencies in our processes. TQ emphasized a whole-company approach to quality. The idea was that every function in the organization—sales, IT, HR, marketing, and so on—played a key role in creating quality for the final customer. Lou had been questioning other senior managers about how P&G could ever monetize what they were learning in the total quality initiative without the involvement of our customers. So with the backing of P&G vice chairman Tom Laco, Lou invited Sam and his senior management team to Cincinnati on February 24–25, 1988, for a two-day customized TQ seminar designed by the famous management guru, W. Edwards Deming.

This time P&G made hotel reservations for the Walmart executives at the historic Queen City Club, but that was way too expensive for Walmart. P&G offered to pay for it, but the Walmart team declined and found another hotel where they stayed two to a room.

The seminar, meanwhile, was a home run. As Lou promised, senior managers from P&G also participated and everyone seemed to buy into the value of a total quality approach. Sam Walton certainly did. When the event came to its end, Sam stood, looked at John Smale, and said, "Let's do this!"

John looked back at him and said, "Let's do what?"

"The TQ thing," Sam said, "between our two companies."

Sam was a man of ready-fire-aim action. P&G was a company that chewed on decisions like they were thick cuts of steak.

John looked at Sam and said, "We'll get back to you."

At my retirement party in 2003, Lee Scott, CEO of Walmart from 2000 to 2009, said attending that TQM meeting was "one of the great thrills in my business career . . . that meeting changed Walmart stores in many ways and made us a better company."

After that seminar, at Lou's insistence, John convened his senior leadership team to talk about how to respond to Sam's offer. Suddenly, the work we'd done on the internal design team came back into play. Lou pushed for P&G to execute the recommendations in our report—create a multifunctional team of P&G folks, move them to Arkansas, and start a collaborative working relationship between the two companies.

There was heavy pushback by most of the senior group, but Lou and Tom Laco prevailed and John Smale, to his great credit, agreed to do a test of a different structure with Walmart based on the general principles from the design team's recommendation. Had John not made this courageous decision, it would have been a huge corporate embarrassment and, in hindsight, an even bigger missed business opportunity.

In April 1988, John Pepper sent an internal memo with what he called the company's "primary statement" about P&G's new "customer beliefs and strategies." This memo, which he urged leaders to consider carefully when developing the "individual strategies for your respective businesses and categories," boiled our original design team findings into five "customer beliefs" and three "strategic principles for better customer relationships."

The general sentiment within much of the senior leadership group, however, was that we would fail—but they could all take credit for trying something new.

I was appointed to lead this experimental team, and a couple of months later Nancy and I were invited to dinner at the home of John and Phyllis Smale. The other guests: Sam and Helen Walton.

In retrospect, this was a brilliant move by John to introduce me as the team lead for P&G, help me establish a relationship with Walmart's founder, and ease any concerns Sam might have about how P&G would approach the partnership.

It gave the impression that I was his hand-picked leader, that I was higher in the organization than I was, that I had his full support, and that I had access to him as needed. It also gave Sam and Helen the opportunity to get to know me and Nancy on a more personal level. They were very engaged as we talked about our Christian mission work in the inner city of Cincinnati, how Nancy had started a school, how we regularly took in foster care children, and how we participated in programs that helped feed the less fortunate.

Later I learned that our dinner discussions at the Smales' was a confidence builder to both Sam and Helen. Sam was expecting that the P&G team leader would be an Ivy League northerner who would see everyone at Walmart as "bumpkins" and expect morning coffee to arrive in a fine china cup.

I was more of a Styrofoam cup kind of guy. Plus, the important role faith played in my life and in Nancy's would be a door-opener at Walmart's headquarters down in the Bible Belt. Many of their senior executives were outspoken followers of Jesus who were active in church, faith-based ministries, and other nonprofits.

I'll talk a good bit about the "deep state" resistance we faced in building our team and growing the partnership with Walmart, but one thing should be clear: the commitment at the very top of the two organizations was vital and never wavered.

John and Phyllis made a return trip to Arkansas to stay with the Waltons in August 1988, which helped them gain a deeper appreciation for Sam, Helen, and Walmart.

"They are two very fine, quality people," Sam wrote of John and Phyllis in a letter to Lou Pritchett. "We enjoyed their visit very much. I think they, too, came to a greater appreciation of our company as well as what both of us are trying to achieve. Hopefully, we will be able to move on and progressively achieve our respective goals."[3]

John also accompanied me to a Walmart Saturday meeting, where he spoke to their entire home office team. This raised P&G's credibility within Walmart, and mine as well. Additionally, John would call me occasionally to get an update and give Sam a call to check in and get his take on our joint progress.

Other top P&G leaders—Lou Pritchett, Tom Laco, Mike Milligan, Gerry Dirvin, and John Pepper, in particular—were instrumental with their support in the early years. And the CEOs who followed Smale—Pepper, Ed Artzt, Durk Jager, and A. G. Lafley—all became active supporters of our work and worked closely with Walmart's CEOs.

Once or twice a year, for instance, the CEOs of the two companies would get together. Sometimes they walked stores together so the Walmart CEO could help the P&G CEO understand how they (and their competitors) executed their strategies. Some of the meetings were in Cincinnati, where the Walmart leader could hear from P&G executives. Through the years, many P&G executives attended Walmart's Saturday morning meetings and their shareholders meetings with me. They typically would arrive a day early and also address the Walmart top talent sessions that meet on Friday afternoons.

Walmart's executives, meanwhile, addressed a variety of P&G groups. Walmart board member and former president and COO Jack Shewmaker, for instance, once spoke at our global annual meeting, which was a first for someone representing one of our retail customers.

When the CEOs got together, they often stayed at the host CEO's home. I'll never forget one dinner I was fortunate to attend when Durk Jager was CEO of P&G and Walmart CEO Lee Scott was visiting. It was a very good evening and Durk showed off his impressive wine cellar to Lee, but the most memorable thing about what became known as "sleepover one" was that Lee forgot to pack his socks. So the next day Durk gave him a pair of socks to wear when he came to the P&G offices.

Sometime later, Lee invited Durk to Bentonville—this was "sleepover two"—and he showed off his fly-fishing equipment after our dinner that night. As far as I know, Durk remembered his socks.

Friendships developed between all of these leaders, and they interacted with each other often, not just in business matters. John Smale and several other P&G executives, for instance, were with me in the auditorium in Bentonville on March 17, 1992, when Sam got the Presidential Medal of Freedom from President George H. W. Bush.

John Pepper and Don Soderquist (president of Walmart Stores) had a particularly rich friendship, and I obviously had good relationships with a number of Walmart executives outside of the business. I was on a board with Ruth Glass (David's wife), served on the Harding University president's board with Walmart CFO Paul Carter, served on the John Brown University board of trustees with Don Soderquist, and was involved in several Christian-related events with Walmart CEO Mike Duke.

But that all would come later. Way back on June 27, 1988, roughly one year after the first canoe trip and a month or two after our dinner at the Smales', Lou Pritchett and Tom Laco joined me for a visit to the Walmart's headquarters in Bentonville, where we worked with their executives to finalize an agreement to test this new concept.

Now the real work for me and my team could begin.

Notes

1. Lou Pritchett, interview with the author, 2023.
2. Pritchett, interview.
3. Sam Walton to Lou Pritchett, August 22, 1988, Lou Pritchett Papers, Box 1, Folder 57, University of Arkansas.

CHAPTER 5

Intentional Design

The recommendations from our internal design team at P&G gave us a useful starting point for figuring out where we might go with Walmart, but, of course, it was short on specifics.

The big ideas in that report would radically disrupt and transform the way Walmart and P&G did business, and that required a more intentionally designed plan. So in August 1988, we brought our multifunctional design team to Bentonville, Arkansas, and began research that was specific to Walmart.

We needed to clearly define the realities we faced, including the roadblocks, expectations, and opportunities. And we needed to start formulating practical solutions for a more productive and collaborative working relationship.

Bill Fields, the head of merchandising for Walmart, coordinated a week of meetings between our ten-member design team and Walmart associates from every function that had any interaction, no matter how indirect, with P&G's business. We also spoke with leaders at different levels. So, for instance, we didn't just talk to a buyer, but to that buyer's supervisor and that supervisor's supervisor.

In those days, Bentonville's population barely topped ten thousand, and there were hardly any restaurants or hotels in the town. So we rented a few condominiums in the nearby town of Bella Vista, a planned community that catered to retirees who played golf, fished, played tennis, and enjoyed other social events with each other.

Each day we drove to the Walmart headquarters, and from 7 a.m. to 5 p.m. we asked our counterparts to outline their responsibilities, explain how they measured success, explain the biggest issues they faced in their work, and describe any specific issues they had in their relationship with P&G.

We asked follow-up questions and drilled as deeply as we could so that we could develop a thorough understanding of the topics we were discussing. Then we'd head back to one of the condominiums, order dinner from Dairy Queen or Fred's Hickory Inn barbecue (our best available options), and spend the evening debriefing the day's findings on a flipchart.

This approach allowed us to build on each other's observations, ensure we were aligned on what we were learning, come up with additional questions for the Walmart team, and record recommendations that might serve as a win for both companies. Our first meeting the next day would be with the same team members we had interviewed the previous day—that way we could ask clarifying questions and seek their input on our ideas.

It made for a grueling week, but it was a highly productive process.

One of our biggest breakthroughs came when we were reviewing the comments from our discussions with Walmart's finance team. During our debrief, Kathy Blair, the P&G finance representative, said one of her takeaways was that Walmart viewed their stores as profit centers. We dutifully noted the comment on the flipchart and moved on to other observations.

About ten minutes later, Kathy spoke up again and said, "I don't think you appreciate the fact that their stores are profit centers." I pointed out that we had captured that point on the flipchart, and we began discussing other functional issues that were specific to the finance department.

Another ten minutes passed and Kathy spoke up again. "You don't understand that their stores are profit centers," she said.

At this point she was starting to sound like a broken record, and I was getting a bit cranky. She could see the frustration and asked if she could take a minute to explain what the rest of us were missing.

When P&G sells products to Walmart, she said, the invoice goes to the company's headquarters, which then charges each store for the products it sells. The store is charged the invoice price, regardless of any discount that might have been involved. And that can make our products less profitable to the stores, which, as she had noted, were profit centers.

The best way to understand the impact of this is with a hypothetical example.

Let's say P&G charged Walmart $10 per item for a product and Walmart marked it up 10 percent and sold it every day for $11. But then

P&G offered a short-term discount of $2 per item sold, allowing Walmart to sell it at $9. This saved the shopper money and improved Walmart's margin.

P&G, however, would then send Walmart a check to pay the $2 per item sold. The store, meanwhile, was still billed $10 per item, so it actually lost $1 on every item sold.

Store managers based their displays and other merchandising decisions on the impact those decisions would have on profits, as well as sales. So our payment policy created a disincentive for stores to sell more of our items, since the more they sold the more money they lost. It also gave them an incentive to sell more of our competitor's products, since those were more profitable to the store's bottom line.

In other words, even when P&G offered Walmart a better deal than our competitor, the competitor's products would get better merchandising treatment because their allowance money was paid off the invoice and they were viewed as more profitable by the stores. If we would just pay the $2 per item off the invoice rather than by check, the stores would be billed $8 per item and earn $1 per sale.

Light bulbs blinked on all throughout the condo, and not just the ones screwed into lamps.

The next day when we had our follow-up meetings with Walmart's finance team, we asked what happened to our allowance money since we paid it as bill-backs. We were told that it went into a buyer's account and the buyer could use it however he or she wanted.

Theoretically, someone said, if our money went into a buyer's account and he decided to spend that money on a competitor's item, would he be free to do that?

The answer: *Yes. That's why it's called the buyer's account.*

Needless to say, we were horrified at the implications of this on our ability to build our business and be competitively priced with our competition.

Many of our customers had been pushing for years to get P&G to pay our allowances off the invoice, but we had resisted. Our allowances were performance-based and we didn't want to pay the money until we had seen the performance. Then we would give them a check for that money.

What we learned that day, thanks to Kathy's persistence, eventually resulted in a test on the Walmart business where we paid our allowances off invoice and then monitored the results to ensure we got the required performance for the allowance money. The test was a terrific success and eventually was expanded more broadly within P&G and to other customers.

We brought a multifunctional team to every meeting and every debrief that week, and the diversity of skills, experiences, and expertise led to robust discussion and unpredictable solutions. And we were able to learn how different decisions and policies had intended and unintended consequences on all the different functions.

We used this process moving forward when we created the cross-functional mirror team because learning and talking about things collectively allowed for a much broader understanding and justification for anything that we might do or recommend. And it also helped us identify much earlier in the process the potential barriers that we'd eventually have to address.

After a full week in Bella Vista and Bentonville, our team loaded up our flipcharts and all the notes we had taken, and we headed back to Cincinnati. But I decided we needed to make a special stop in Fayetteville on our way to the airport.

John Molter, a design team member from the United Kingdom, had drawn attention to himself all week when it came to our meals. For one thing, people found it interesting that he used his knife and fork simultaneously when he ate. For another, he consistently lamented over the food we ate when we were in the condos. He wanted at least one "proper" sit-down breakfast before we left, so we stopped at a restaurant in Fayetteville where he could get one.

And what do you think John ordered? Cornflakes. How's that for a proper English breakfast?

John, by the way, also recalls sitting at Sam Walton's desk on our first day at the Walmart home office. He had his feet on the desk, in fact, when Sam walked in.

"He was very gracious after my apology," John told me at the time. "'No problem. Thanks for visiting with us,' was his reply."

Once we were back in Cincinnati, we turned our general recommendations into more specific recommendations for establishing a first-of-its-kind multifunctional team from P&G that would work directly with a customer, which in this case would be Walmart.

This team, we said, shouldn't include just members of our sales force, but all functions. The team needed to be located near the customer—in or close to Bentonville, in this case. And it should be empowered with decision-making ability and the flexibility to create some learning lab approaches to determine the best ways to build the joint business.

The team leaders also should have smaller offices than they had in other P&G locations and share administrative assistants to reduce costs and promote teamwork. The smaller offices would align better with Walmart's culture than the much bigger offices we would have had in Cincinnati.

I spent the rest of that year working on the details, mainly regarding budgeting, staffing, and year-one strategies and goals for what would become a sink-or-swim test case for the one-company operating model. And then we presented our case to all the functional leaders at P&G's headquarters, as well as to leaders at Walmart.

These presentations included two primary objectives: grow the business with Walmart (in both volume and profitability) across all categories and invent a new method of doing business that P&G could expand to other key customers. The latter was the more radical of the two, because it involved developing a multifunctional approach with a team located near the customer.

Our proposal also included working versions of strategies, key measures of success, an outline of how we would report status and progress updates, a basic business plan with some audacious goals (achieving $1 billion in sales to Walmart within three years, for instance), and a list of tactics for achieving those goals.

There was plenty of resistance to the proposed changes. Some leaders had legitimate concerns. For instance, would a team based near the customer and intent on collaborating with that customer be tempted to put the customer's interests ahead of P&G's interests? And would the proposed new approach add to the complexities and costs of doing business?

Others were understandably fearful of the unknowns and the impact things like changes to the traditional reporting structures might have on their lives and their business units. And, to be totally transparent, a few simply dug in their heels in defense of the status quo. They thought it was a dumb idea and would never work.

We had the backing of Lou Pritchett, Tom Laco, John Pepper, and, most importantly, CEO John Smale, and we eventually gained approval to put the plan into action. But we also worked hard to seek input from all the functions that would be affected, develop strategies that were good for the overall business, and communicate consistent messages about the benefits for both companies. We didn't want to force the buy-in, we wanted to earn it.

We approached that in much the same way we approached those initial meetings at the Walmart home office—by listening with an effort to understand, by looking for common ground, and by clearly illustrating the benefits of the changes we were proposing.

Would the skeptics and doubters ever buy into the idea that we could make these changes a reality? Most would and a few wouldn't. But within a few months of that trip to Bentonville, Sam Walton helped us send a clear and strong message that P&G's relationship with Walmart had found its way into new territory.

CHAPTER 6

Shooting Birds, Hitting Pringles

My goal was simple: don't kill one of Sam Walton's dogs.

Ordinarily, those dogs had nothing to fear from me, but ordinarily I don't walk around with a loaded shotgun in my hands. In January 1989, however, I roamed the fields of Sam and Bud Walton's South Texas ranch to do something I'd never done in my life—hunt birds. And given my level of skill and experience, the bird dogs had more reason to be nervous than the quail.

Lou Pritchett, Tom Laco, and I were there largely because Sam Walton decided to use the gathering to send a message about the budding collaborative partnership between Walmart and P&G.

As P&G's freshly appointed team leader for the initiative, I had been to Walmart's headquarters in Arkansas several times in the six months since Lou, Tom, and I made our initial trip in June 1988. I was getting to know the people of Walmart and how they operated, and by late in 1988 some members of the P&G team we were forming were already working at least part time in Arkansas. But while we had made considerable progress on plans for the partnership, one thing had become clear: we needed buy-in, alignment, and support from every level of the two organizations or this thing would never work.

Many of the Walmart associates and executives who had worked on the P&G business were reluctant to believe there would be any meaningful change in our operating methods. Who could blame them? Their expectations were based on the realities they had experienced for years. And, as I've mentioned already, P&G had doubters who didn't think the concept would work and resisters who actively opposed it.

We built support in several ways over the years, and I'll share some of those tactics in subsequent chapters. In the meantime, I can't overstate the importance of having the support of the leaders at the top of both organizations. They made that support known with words and with actions, and Sam made a highly visible demonstration of his commitment by inviting the three of us to hunt quail with his leadership team.

Sam and his brother, Bud, leased thousands of acres of land in South Texas, and they used it often to combine business meetings with quail hunting. But they had never invited outsiders—just friends, family, and other Walmart associates.

Our presence on this trip sent a message that echoed like a shotgun blast throughout both companies. Sam was inviting three P&G leaders— the head of national sales (Lou), a vice-chairman (Tom), and little old me—into what most considered an inner-circle event.

Bud had built a large stone house on the property with all the conveniences of modern life, including a cook who made bacon and egg breakfasts for those guests. But Sam preferred more spartan quarters. He had a few old trailers where guests could sleep and one that was set up as a place to eat. Breakfast was coffee and Otis Spunkmeyer muffins from Sam's Club.

As Sam's guests, we stayed in the trailers, where each of us bunked with one of the Walmart executives. I shared a trailer with Don Soderquist, while Tom Laco was with Sam, and Lou was with Rob Walton (Sam's son and vice-chair of Walmart's board).

"Now here I am, about to retire, never fired a shotgun before," Lou recalled. "And there's Rob Walton, who was preparing to run in the Iron Man contest where you run and swim and bike for miles. And here we were sleeping six feet apart in a trailer in Falfurrias, Texas. I said, 'Oh my God, how will I ever get out of this?' So I did the best I could to go to sleep. But I don't think it really worked."[1]

The Walmart executives, of course, were experienced hunters, whereas I had to borrow a shotgun and go to a range to learn how to shoot it (which I did rather poorly).

In preparation for the trip, I also bought some hunting clothes—a jacket that was briar proof, special hunting pants, rattlesnake guards that looked like gear for a professional baseball catcher, and a hat with a feather that would have made Robin Hood green with envy.

Everyone else wore jeans, T-shirts, and ball caps. I'm pretty sure some of them had cigarettes rolled up in their shirt sleeves and cans of Skoal in their pockets.

When it was time to hunt, we broke into groups that consisted of three hunters, a dog handler, and three dogs. Our group loaded into a pickup and drove to an assigned location somewhere in the middle of thirty-one square miles of prairie grass and mesquite trees.

The dog handler—a John Wayne type with large, calloused hands, a cowboy hat, and an intimidating presence—took the dogs out and let them go. As the dogs flushed out the quail, the hunters followed in a line behind them.

I was paired with Paul Carter, Walmart's CFO, and Bill Hutchinson, who owned shoe stores and had partnered with Sam to put them in some of his original stores. I figured they were evaluating me and would give Sam a report, but I was way more concerned about not shooting those dogs than about what they might say about me. While Paul and Bill aimed skyward to the left or right to lead the quail, I mostly aimed up or down and straight ahead, and I seldom pulled the trigger when it wasn't on safety.

In three days of hunting, I made a lot of noise and somehow managed to kill the four unluckiest quail in the world. They had to have flown into the path where I was shooting, because there was no way I was good enough to shoot them in flight!

Despite my modest results as a hunter, the trip was highly successful for our partnership efforts. Just being invited increased my credibility throughout Walmart. And at night we sat around the campfire and talked about a variety of subjects, including business.

The Walmart executives got to know us, we got a deeper sense of the Walmart culture and the camaraderie on their team, and I even learned some new expressions that we could add to our team's lexicon. When someone heard an idea that resonated with them, for instance, they would say, "That dog will hunt!" That was something I'd never heard prior to the trip, but something I said many times afterward.

The Walmart leaders seemed to enjoy it as much as we did.

"We certainly enjoyed having you join us for our 'great hunting expedition' in South Texas," Don Soderquist wrote in a letter to me about a month after the event. "It's fun to relax, let down your hair, break bread together and bunk in old trailers with business associates and partners. It's wonderful to see how far our joint venture in the unique business relationship has progressed. I believe that we've only just begun to see the results of a true commitment in trust."[2]

Don hit on something powerful in that letter. The Walmart-P&G journey would become an exercise in building trust. More than twenty years
before Stephen M. R. Covey would write *The Speed of Trust,* Don already
knew that business was done primarily through relationships, and that
trust was foundational for all relationships.

We had to build trust internally at P&G, and we had to build trust
with our counterparts throughout Walmart. We had to consistently demonstrate our capabilities and our character, as Covey put it, and every
interaction became a brick in the bridge to trust.

It was also during the three-day hunting trip that I took a risk and
made a promise I knew I couldn't keep without some divine intervention
that some within P&G would have thought as unlikely as the parting of
the Red Sea.

Walmart's executives had an annual competition with each other
where each picked a product that would become their VPI—volume
producing item. The products sponsored by the executives got extra displays, price reductions, and other merchandising incentives for a full year,
with the idea being that these products would draw shoppers into their
stores and result in greater overall sales.

The executives earned points based on units sold, total sales (in dollars), and gross profits (in dollars), and, of course, each executive wanted
his product to perform the best. They shared the results every Saturday
morning during their meetings at Walmart's home office and bragging
rights were earned or lost.

"I want you to give me a P&G item that will be my VPI for the year,"
Sam told me during one of the breaks in the hunting.

Sam, of course, was a world-class merchant and had considerable sway
over how products were sold, so he was hard to beat in this competition.
The previous year, in fact, he had won with Moon Pies as his VPI. So the
pressure was on to give him an item that would keep him in the winner's
circle.

I figured if I was going to put all my chips on the table on this gamble,
I might as well go with Pringles, the stackable potato chips P&G invented in the 1960s. For it to qualify as Sam's item, however, we would
have to agree to a fixed price on a can of the chips for an entire year.
Sam would then set a retail price for customers and keep that in place
for a year.

Well, this was a huge problem on several levels. First, I didn't have the authority to make item cost decisions for any product division. And second, having one price for the year was the opposite of the P&G merchandising practices. We used a high-low pricing strategy, which meant we offered a special allowance for price reduction and merchandising of an item during parts of the year while selling it at a higher price with no allowance the rest of the year.

Furthermore, we had a policy that all promotional allowances were available to all customers under the same conditions; there was no preferential treatment to one customer over another.

I knew this was going to be extremely difficult to sell within P&G, but I also knew it would be an important first test of my authority level and the willingness of P&G to change. Plus, I needed to make a commitment to Sam while on the trip rather than saying, "I'll get back to you."

I outlined the situation with Tom Laco and Lou Pritchett, and they agreed to provide the cover for me back in Cincinnati. Tom Laco, for instance, said he would speak directly with the vice president of the food division to get an exception to the normal promotion policy so we could participate in the VPI program with Pringles as Sam's item for the year.

On the last night of the hunting trip, Sam proudly announced that Pringles would be his VPI for the coming year. His team was surprised, but also curious to see how this would play out, because they knew all too well that I, on behalf of P&G, had just committed to something we had never done with Walmart.

Predictably, we returned to Cincinnati to finalize the details, and all hell broke loose. After a great deal of high-spirited debate, however, we reached an agreement for a test on one item for one year with the condition that whatever we offered Walmart would be the average price available to every other customer in the market on the high-low pricing system.

I sent Sam a letter a few weeks after the hunting trip with the details of our proposal, which I conservatively estimated would help Walmart sell at least a million cases of Pringles in a year. Furthermore, I estimated he would earn more than thirty million points in the VPI, which would be twenty million more points than Moon Pies earned the previous year.

Pringles was an enormous success as a VPI, and Sam had a lot of fun for the year with his other executives. He also clearly sent a message to his organization that P&G was willing to change but that it would require work from both P&G and Walmart to bring about the high potential of this new relationship.

For the partnership to thrive, however, we had to produce more than a one-off success on a promotional item. We had to go to Arkansas and grow our team and the relationship. And what better place to start than underneath a flower shop?

Notes

1. Lou Pritchett, interview with the author, 2023.
2. Don Soderquist to the author, February 16, 1989 (author's personal collection).

PART II

One Team, One Dream

People need to know what the end goal looks like, what they are trying to accomplish, and why the dream is worth it. In the early stage of the relationship between Walmart and P&G, we had to devote tremendous effort to designing new ways of working that supported the vision. Without the vision, people perish. Change will perish.

CHAPTER 7

Setting Up Shop

On January 10, 1989, the P&G executive committee announced eight new positions in the General Sales Department, and I officially became "Director, Customer Business Development"—or, as they would say in Arkansas, *director of customer bidness development.*

"In this capacity," the announcement read, "Mr. Muccio will have overall responsibility for the Wal-Mart Customer Team, which includes multifunctional management of the Company's business with Wal-Mart, Inc."[1]

The others listed in the announcement were Don Bechtel (product supply), Kathy Blair (finance), Brad Simpson (store operations), Bill Toler (marketing), John Molter (special assignment), and David Hollenbeck (technology manager).

This formed the nucleus of our original Walmart Customer Team as we moved from the planning stages toward the creation of a truly multifunctional, on-site operation. But obviously we needed to bring in additional talent, and we needed a place to work as close to the Walmart home office in Bentonville as possible.

The metropolitan statistical area of Northwest Arkansas is now home to around six hundred thousand residents. There are hundreds of great restaurants and plenty of hotels. There's a world-class art museum, miles of hiking and biking trails, and performance venues that bring in A-list recording artists and the hottest Broadway shows.

While cow pastures and chicken farms surround the regional airport, it is a short drive away from Bentonville or Fayetteville and is served by all the major airlines and a few discount carriers.

In 1989, however, the metro population was only ninety-five thousand and the closest commercial airport to Walmart's headquarters was nearly an hour's drive away on the southern edge of Fayetteville, home of the University of Arkansas and the cultural center of the region.

The flights on the propeller-powered puddle-hoppers that flew there often were delayed or canceled due to thick fog on a runway that was nestled tightly between mountain ridges. As I came to say, you couldn't buy a ticket to Fayetteville, you could only buy a chance.

When it came to establishing a beachhead in the area, our options were limited. The only office space available in Bentonville was in strip malls and empty warehouses that lacked the security required by P&G's real estate division. Fayetteville had far more options, so we went there and rented a place near the downtown square while we searched for a more long-term solution.

Thus, the first home of the P&G pioneers was in a basement underneath a flower shop.

We knew all along that those would be temporary offices, but we were there long enough for Sam Walton to pay us a memorable call.

Harry Campbell and Mike Graen were among those in the office that day. Harry had given up a role in advertising in Cincinnati to take a newly created sales role representing the health care part of the P&G portfolio. And Mike, who was married with two young children, was our first functional lead in information technology.

"We had maybe three or four offices with very flimsy walls in between," Harry recalled. "We had a big copier about the size of Mount Everest, and we had a bunch of file drawers. We were in there one day chatting and laughing about something when all of a sudden standing at the door was this gentleman. It was Sam Walton."[2]

This visit proved helpful to our team in multiple ways. For starters, this was Sam's type of office—not too different from Walmart's home offices in its early days. The décor looked like it had come from a yard sale, and he appreciated the idea that we were doing all we could to keep our costs down.

Sam chatted with our team for a few minutes and asked how things were going, especially with the efforts to relocate people to the area. Someone mentioned that the team wasn't having much success getting mortgages for homes. Mike Graen and his wife, for instance, had made an offer on a home but hadn't yet arranged the financing.

Sam picked up a phone and made a call to the president of McIlroy Bank, which had operated in the region for more than a hundred years and at that time was owned by Jim Walton's Arvest Bank Group. Jim, of course, is Sam Walton's son.

"I didn't know what was happening," Harry told me, "but I had this vision that at that bank there were a whole lot of people suddenly doing a whole lot of stuff to try to help out the P&G folks."[3]

Harry and his wife, by the way, had already purchased a home in Fayetteville, and later he learned that a picture of their yellow house was on a bulletin board in the office of P&G CEO John Pepper. It was a symbolic reminder to John of the commitment the multifunctional team members were making in this experiment.

Around a dozen P&G team members moved to Arkansas in late 1988 and early 1989, but several of us maintained offices in Cincinnati—in an annex across the street from the main headquarters. Don Bechtel, our product supply leader, and I were the last two of the original team members to relocate to Arkansas, moving in 1990 after we'd done what was needed in Cincinnati to help recruit team members and set up support systems within the home office.

Initially, we also had team members located in other parts of the country. Henry Ho, for instance, worked from Dallas for around eighteen months while consolidating all the order processing and customer service functions from across five different offices into one unit that he eventually brought to Arkansas to serve Walmart.

No matter where we were located, we all regularly converged on Arkansas during those first few years—even if we had to spend the night in the St. Louis airport as part of the journey.

Bill Toler was a key player in the move for P&G, because he served as the top on-the-ground lieutenant in Arkansas. In addition to his business experience, Bill was familiar with the area. His father-in-law had earned a degree from the University of Arkansas. Bill and his wife, Melanie, had both attended middle school in Little Rock, Arkansas, and they also had attended Texas A&M, a rival of the UA in sports.

When we approached him about the position, however, Bill had just moved for the third time in eighteen months and Melanie had secured a good job in Cincinnati. He wasn't eager to pull up their roots again.

After reviewing a report on our plans during their Christmas vacation, he and Melanie recognized that the Walmart Customer Service Team was a leading-edge project and that he was a good fit to help it succeed. So they devised a plan that would allow him to take the position with our team.

They bought a home in Fayetteville, furnished it at their own expense, joined the country club, and engaged in the community, but they also kept their home in Cincinnati so Melanie could keep her job there. On the weekends, he would fly back to Ohio or his wife would come to Arkansas.

They paid their own expenses for the commute, but we did our best to help them out. We often scheduled meetings in Cincinnati on Mondays, for instance, so Bill could have more time there and write off the flights as a legitimate business expense. But they treated Arkansas like home, not like a temporary assignment.

"It was very important to both my wife and to me that people knew Fayetteville was our community," Bill told me. "That's why we joined the country club and got involved in things in the area. And it was really important to me that the team knew I was there and committed to being the team leader on the ground. That's the way you positioned the job in the beginning: I was the team leader on the ground and you were the team leader in Cincinnati fighting those battles."[4]

Bill established relationships for P&G with banks, real estate agents, insurance agents, and anyone else who could help smooth the transition for our team members, and he took the lead in training and managing our team in Arkansas.

Those of us still based in Cincinnati worked to identify and recruit talent, and Bill helped recruit and then trained them to operate in ways that were totally new for most of them. Regardless of their role—sales, marketing, brand management, IT, finance, HR, or logistics—they needed to think holistically about how P&G and Walmart operated and help create solutions across multifunctional areas.

Bill recalled an early meeting he had in Dallas with around eleven salespeople who regularly called on Walmart buyers but in some cases had never even met each other. We wanted them all to move to Arkansas. Only two, Tom Verdery and Bill Currie, said yes. That left us, Bill Toler in particular, with several roles to fill.

"My job became talking to each one of the national sales managers and saying, 'I need a person to represent your business in Fayetteville,'" Bill told me. "But where it got complicated was they were going to report to me and I was reporting to you as the team leader. So they were going to lose control, and that's where the friction first began. In the end, we were all on the same team, but it took a lot of effort to convince people that [our] success was fully based upon growing their division's business at Walmart faster than what had been done before. Walmart was growing well with everybody at that point in time. It's just that it was growing much slower than it should have."[5]

Some leaders at P&G headquarters saw the importance of the business and encouraged their top talent to make the move, but it wasn't always an easy sell. A few people we wanted on the team weren't willing to take the risk of what they considered a tour of duty in the backwoods of Arkansas. Others turned us down because they were rooted in the communities where they lived.

It was our job, especially early in the team's formation, to sell recruits on our vision, so we looked for top talent that we thought would appreciate the adventure of doing something new and then we made our pitch.

For instance, in 1991 we identified Jesse Edelman as a rising star who could help us analyze all the data we were starting to get from Walmart. When Jesse's manager in Cincinnati told him of our interest in having him join our team, however, we had a few things working against us.

One, Jesse already had been offered a role in New York, where (two) his girlfriend at the time happened to live and where (three) a young Jewish man would likely feel more at home than in the Ozark Mountains of Arkansas.

"I said, 'I don't think I'm going to do that,'" Jesse recalled.[6]

The manager convinced him to take a look, so he booked a commercial flight to Arkansas. Our team had a charter flight that happened to be making the trip the same day Jesse was coming, and I happened to be on that flight. So I called him and suggested he join me on the charter flight.

"I got on the charter and you were no more than six feet across from me," Jesse recalled. "And you spent the next two-plus hours pulling stuff out of your briefcase to show me all the communications and how important it all was. I mean, you had the hard sell on me for a solid two hours. And I don't know that I've ever recovered from that conversation."[7]

When we landed, I took him to the softball field where our company team was playing and got him in the game. He spent the evening hanging out with some of the single members of our team, and the next day we continued to roll the red carpet until eventually he agreed to a two-year commitment on the team.

"By the time I was done, I had drunk every bit of the Kool-Aid that was poured into me," he said. "But it all started on that plane ride."[8]

Jesse was a perfect fit for our team; all he needed was a good reason to join the P&G counterculture.

"It was very much an us against the man sort of thing, you know, kind of fighting bureaucracy with everything that we did," Jesse said. "And a lot of what we did was a little unconventional in the eyes of what P&G would consider to be conventional approaches or conventional culture."[9]

We also had to sell people on benefits that went beyond their careers or the greater good of the company. We also had to convince them that they could thrive in a small-town community—that the schools would be good for their children, that their trailing spouse could find a job, or that they would have something fun to do if they were single.

Nancy Biddle, a lifelong resident of Fayetteville and one of the nicest, sweetest southern-talking women you'd ever want to meet, played an important role in these efforts.

When we had people come down for a look-see trip, Nancy typically showed them around the community and addressed whatever issues they had. If they had a special-needs child, she introduced them to support services. If they were interested in a faith-based school, she arranged visits so they could see their options.

We also had arrangements with several real estate firms so recruits could see some of the typical houses in various price ranges. And someone on the existing team would host them for dinner one of the nights while they were here so they could learn firsthand about our culture and feel more comfortable in making the decision to join the team.

Eventually, we landed some proven superstars and some team members who were big on enthusiasm and potential but low on experience. Several of those turned into superstars. And, of course, we got a few who were available but simply weren't qualified.

One of the superstars Providence provided was Jeff Schomburger, who came aboard around the middle of 1989. The person we had hired to handle sales for paper products didn't work out, and Bill Toler was exploring options to fill that position.

Jeff, who already had a reputation as a top salesman, had taken a leave to attend graduate school, but then changed his mind and wanted to return to work. His old spot had already been filled, so he couldn't go back to that role. We were happy to have him on our team, and it worked out OK for him, too, because he took my place as team leader when I retired at the end of 2003.

Most members of our early team were drawn by the challenge and the vision of what we were trying to accomplish. As John Green, one of our first analysts on the team, recalled, our pitch was that "we're going to do something that's never been done before."[10]

That was appealing to new team members, but they came knowing that an assignment on the Walmart Customer Team was a bit of a risk to their career and might not be easy on their personal lives. There definitely were pros and cons to making the move, depending on each person's unique situation.

The University of Arkansas provided a plus. It offered quality higher education for those who wanted to pursue an advanced degree, entertainment with the Razorbacks' sports teams, and a willing partner for research that would result in all sorts of innovations in retail best practices and supply chain management.

Most of the nonacademic working professionals in the area, however, were bankers, lawyers, physicians, and owners of small businesses. With the exceptions of Walmart in Bentonville, J. B. Hunt Transport in Lowell, and Tyson Foods in Springdale, there weren't many other employees of large corporations in the region.

There also were very few non-Christians, very few African Americans, very few single professional women, and very few high-end jobs for trailing spouses. And there was a shortage of high-end housing, although the housing that was available was much less expensive per square foot than in larger cities.

All of the pioneers made sacrifices to make the move, but I always thought it was particularly challenging for the women on the team.

Kathy Blair, our first finance manager, was single but dating someone in Cincinnati when she moved down with no guarantees that we would succeed. Ramona Kent, young and single, took a newly invented operations role. Ella Smiley and Kim Hensley were the first administrative assistants who transferred in, Ella from Kansas City and Kim from Tulsa.

And then there was Pam Killingsworth, a single mother with two young children living in Dallas who moved to Northwest Arkansas and was a key player in establishing our continuous improvement process.

In many ways, however, the small-town atmosphere also worked to our advantage. Everyone on the team got to know each other well, from the names of their kids and dogs to the activities they enjoyed, and that promoted a family attitude environment that revealed itself in the ways we would offer support when someone hit one of the speed bumps of life.

Like settlers in the historical sense, the team banded together and supported each other in ways that probably would not have happened had we been in a large city.

Mike Graen was particularly helpful when it came to being helpful. Mike was our very own MacGyver! He engineered all sorts of work-arounds in the P&G and Walmart systems to provide data and support, and I'll get into some of those later. But he also was a key culture builder. When new team members arrived, Mike would do everything from unloading their moving truck, to making them furniture, to hooking up their appliances, and, of course, he helped them in the office as well.

Everyone adjusted quickly and soon began to appreciate all that their new community had to offer. Over time, we embraced the benefits of a slower pace, less traffic, shorter commutes, more time with family, and the simple pleasure of strolling around the farmer's market on a Saturday morning. Some even became Razorback fans and learned to "call the Hogs."

"It really gets in your blood because it's a great place to live," Harry Campbell told me of his time in Northwest Arkansas. "It's got great weather. It's got great people. There's a lot of opportunity. And it's a college town. If you love sports, you've got that. You've really got it all covered, and people stayed as a result of it."[11]

Northwest Arkansas appreciated P&G, as well, because we brought an infusion of talented, highly educated workers with above-average incomes who all had a desire to engage in their new community. We were good for the local economy, the schools, the churches, and many other organizations.

That impact grew larger and larger as our team expanded. After a few months beneath the flower shop, Bill managed our move to the IBM building near the Northwest Arkansas Mall. We were able to rent half of the fourth floor—about 6,600 square feet—but we quickly outgrew it, too. By May 1990, Bill was overseeing the construction of a 15,000-square-foot P&G office building on Millsap Road.

"George Faucette was doing most of our real estate at that time," Bill told me. "And he said, 'Hey, I can get an option for you on the land next door to that new space.' I said, 'Yeah, go ahead, but there's not much likelihood of us ever needing that.' And then before we finished the first building, we had already exercised the option to build another building on land next to the first one."[12]

The area around that first office building is well developed now with restaurants, hotels, and other office buildings. Back then it was mostly pastureland, so our only neighbors were a small herd of cattle. We used to joke that this was the only P&G office in the world where the bull was on the outside!

P&G eventually outgrew the two buildings on Millsap, and it now operates from a nearby two-story office with more than sixty thousand square feet of space. In 1989, however, we were still trying to figure out if it made sense to unpack our bags. And based on those early mirror team meetings, not many folks were ready to stick their bags in storage.

Notes

1. Executive Committee announcement, January 10, 1989.
2. Harry Campbell, interview with the author, 2023.
3. Campbell, interview.
4. Bill Toler, interview with the author, 2023.
5. Toler, interview.
6. Jesse Edelman, interview with the author, 2023.
7. Edelman, interview.
8. Edelman, interview.
9. Edelman, interview.
10. John Green, interview with the author, 2023.
11. Campbell, interview.
12. Toler, interview.

CHAPTER 8

Building the Bike Path

One of the great things about letters from Sam Walton was the way they inevitably left you feeling like you were winning whatever battle you thought you faced.

I received a few of those letters through the years, and I've seen several more that he wrote to other people. I can't recall any that didn't include a word of thanks or that weren't encouraging.

If you only read Sam's letters about our new collaboration, however, you might think everything about this new way of doing business fell quickly and neatly into place and that our success was inevitable.

In May 1989, for instance, Sam wrote a letter to P&G CEO John Smale that reflected his gratitude for our progress and his optimism for the initiative.

"It seems to me that things are going real well with your folks down here and I feel we are improving our relationships and doing better things for each other all the time," Sam told John. "I will do the best I can to keep my finger on it and I know you will, as well."[1]

The letter also noted how pleased Sam was that Walmart had honored P&G the previous weekend with a Partners in Excellence Award. John Smale couldn't be there because he was in Europe, but Tom Laco, Lou Pritchett, and a few others joined me at the Walmart home office when the award was handed out during their Saturday morning meeting.

We'd come a long way since the days when Sam couldn't get anyone at P&G to take his call!

Meanwhile, the day after Sam wrote that letter, Walmart and P&G executives signed a confidential disclosure agreement that essentially blessed the collaboration and allowed sensitive information to flow in both directions. This agreement was a huge sign within both companies about the level of expectations and support from senior executives.

Looking back at it, the simplicity of the agreement also illustrates the level of trust already developing between the two companies. The document covered five points and only took up about half a page. It was so clearly written that you have to wonder if any lawyers were even involved. The key point: "to hold all such received information in confidence and to not disclose it to any third party, nor use it for the benefit of any other person or business."

Certainly, we were making progress, but we were mostly plowing fertile ground. We had arranged for a few deals like the Pringles promotion, and we had a general plan for what we wanted to do going forward. Yet we hadn't proved a thing.

"What we've accomplished so far can't yet qualify as a path to the future, but it is a first footprint in the snow," I told an audience of internal P&G leaders in July 1989. "We're exploring; we keep opening new doors. Any assessment of 'success' as a measure against traditional goals at this stage would be invalid. It is history that must judge."

In top-to-top meetings, Sam Walton liked to point out that we had a tendency to make things too complicated. "It should be simple," he would remind us. "You send me products and I send you money." That mantra resonated with our team for years. But the perception among some that "to think it is to do it" just wasn't accurate. It wasn't that easy.

"The individual pieces aren't hard," I told that audience, "but there were very many of them and they are all related. Moreover, the structures of the relationships themselves won't stand still: the people involved are changing, the environment is changing, the customers are changing, and the customers' environments are changing."

To develop a long-term partnership in such a dynamic landscape, we had to move beyond visionary planning and dive into the details on things like our joint operating principles and processes.

This type of collaborative relationship would require unprecedented levels of openness and trust. We not only had to define the roles and expectations of P&G and Walmart, we had to figure out how a team of functional leaders from two companies would execute collaboratively as one company and how we would resolve the inevitable issues that would emerge.

That brings us back to the earliest gatherings of the mirror team.

As I noted in chapter 1, the mirror team consisted of Walmart and P&G leaders and everyone had a functional counterpart from the other company—someone who "mirrored" his or her role. By bringing representatives of all the stakeholders together, we believed we could figure out the best process for working together and develop a broad sense of ownership and commitment to the initiative.

Successful collaboration requires that both parties see that what they're being requested to do will in some way satisfy their own company's interests. The members of the multifunctional mirror team knew the challenges we faced, and they were the right people to solve them. Then they could share with others how those solutions would benefit their function, the two companies, and consumers.

I would often remind P&G audiences that one of the huge benefits of this multifunctional collaboration is that it commercialized the entire company and allowed them to see their "fingerprints" on the results. When we started, only sales, accounts payable, and a few folks in distribution had any interactions with our retail customers. Now, people from packaging, R&D, marketing, and many other functions worked with Walmart and could see firsthand how their jobs directly made a difference in the financial results of P&G.

The first mirror team meeting in the summer of 1989 went smoothly, but it wasn't until our two-day meeting on August 22–23 that we began going deep into the most significant pain points of the relationship.

"At the time, it felt like a root canal without novocaine," recalled Mike Graen, one of the P&G team members. "It was just painful because we wanted to talk about process, total quality, flow charts, and Gant charts, while Walmart was saying things like, 'Can we talk about how painful you are to work with?' They just wanted to get down to the nitty gritty, which was, 'We don't like you guys. You're a pain in the butt to deal with. Every time I ask a question, I get a different answer. You always have to check with somebody when I just need the decision.'"[2]

That's when our process guy, Al Lennon, abandoned the process and shifted to the sticky notes that put in writing all the things that were really broken in the P&G and Walmart relationship. And when we finished, as you might remember, I went to my hotel, called my wife, and jokingly told her we shouldn't unpack when we moved here.

We all left that first day discouraged, but difficult times often prepare people to do great things, and that turned out to be the case with the mirror team. When we returned the next day, we had no choice but to face all those sticky notes and do something about them. If we didn't, they would linger and fester until they killed our chances of success. Instead, we aligned not only on the pain points but on a viable path forward to alleviate them.

Personally, I can't help but credit Providence with playing a hand in what happened. We were on such different pages and had such different mindsets when we walked in, yet we emerged with something that was, in my opinion, brilliant.

I didn't say that I was brilliant or that any of us were brilliant, but the results were brilliant. Even with more than thirty-five years of hindsight, I'm not sure I could improve on any of the outcomes of that meeting.

What were the outcomes?

Among other things, we created a robust set of operating principles, focus areas, and initial objectives, as well as a reverse bowtie visual that became a great communication tool for illustrating how our approach to working together would differ from approaches of the past.

Those outcomes are important, and I'll talk more about them going forward. But it's worth pausing to reflect on why we were in a position to produce lemonade from the buckets of lemons we identified.

- We all knew and agreed on the big-picture vision, which was to work more cooperatively so that both companies could improve their business results and better serve consumers. And this vision for a one-company operating model had the full support of top leaders like Sam Walton and John Smale.
- We had clearly identified the pain points, and we had the sticky notes to prove it. These weren't just about processes and tactics, but about how we treated each other—the things that matter the most when building trust in a relationship.
- We all came to the meeting with good intentions. Some of the groundwork for building trust had been laid through previous meetings— the earlier meeting of the full mirror team and some gatherings that involved sub-teams (like marketing). We weren't sure how things would work, and some had doubts about whether it could, but by this point we knew each other well enough to know we all wanted to do our best to figure it out.

Any multifunctional teams that are attempting a collaboration effort will face similar situations and can follow a similar path forward. Then you have to do what you've said you will do over time, because that's how deep, meaningful, and transformational trust develops.

In the early stages, however, you need to do the same thing you should do when you are casually dating someone and it takes a turn toward something more serious—you need a DTR conversation. You know: "define the relationship."

The mirror team meeting was one big DTR conversation.

The reverse bowtie illustration turned out to be a great visual representation of what the relationship looked like and what we wanted it to look like moving forward. It was not only helpful with our teams but with explaining what we were trying to accomplish when presenting it to other stakeholders across the two organizations.

A normal bowtie looks like two triangles with their widest areas on the outside and the points meeting at the knot in the middle (Figure 8.1).

In the traditional retailer-supplier relationship, the points represent where the buyer (for the retailer) and seller (for the supplier) come together. Behind them in the wider parts of the triangles are all the other people who are involved in the relationship but who never actually interact with each other—the people in finance, logistics, analytics, information technology, as well as executives who set long-term organizational goals and strategies.

Instead, the two people in the middle, who usually have very little decision-making authority, share information back into their organization or they get information from inside their organization and share it with the one person in the middle for the other organization. In that model, the best questions often go unasked, ideas aren't considered, and information is diluted, butchered, or lost as it works its way through the process.

The multifunctional mirror team approach flipped that model to create a reverse bowtie (Figure 8.2). Now the two widest areas were the connection spot in the middle, and information and decisions flowed directly between the experts, were vetted in multifunctional conversations, and then were communicated out toward the points.

The mirror team exemplified the reverse bowtie model. It allowed the people from Walmart to talk with the people from P&G in the context of

Figure 8.1. The Traditional Model

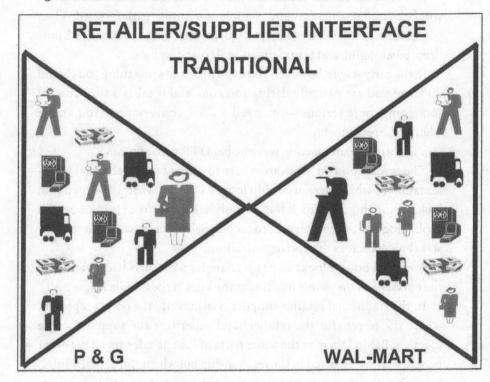

what they were trying to achieve, and that allowed them to identify pain points and, more importantly, solutions. And because the mirror team was cross-functional, members could weigh in on how ideas from one function might have a positive or negative impact on another.

This approach allowed us to align on our one-company operating principles, focus areas, and initial objectives. Functional counterparts would still meet with each other independently of the larger group to work on improved processes and collaborate on strategic plans, but they would do so with a commitment to a common set of principles and focus areas.

The operating principles were grouped into three categories: those involving leadership focus and business results, those involving how we would work, and those involving team interactions. Each category had five to seven bullet points.

For instance, one principle under "leadership focus and business results" was the commitment to improve the profitability of both com-

Figure 8.2. The Reverse Bowtie Model

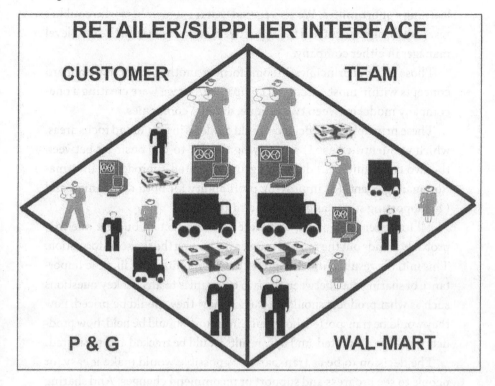

panies by maximizing opportunities and eliminating unnecessary expenses. But that commitment had a caveat: we wouldn't pursue anything we knew would be a detriment to the ultimate consumer.

Another commitment in this category was an acknowledgment that we were the advocates for each other within our companies—the Walmart members would advocate for P&G within Walmart and vice versa—but that we ultimately would support the decisions of our own company.

Under "how we work," we committed to honoring confidentiality when it came to sensitive data, to trusting each other's commitment to do the right thing, to consulting each other on key decisions, to dealing with disagreements as "business issues" rather than "personal issues," and to taking responsibility for our work.

The "team interaction" category included everything from acknowledging that we had the freedom to challenge existing ways of thinking and working to defining the fifty-fifty split of joint expenses to maintaining a "correction of errors" file so that mistakes could become learning opportunities. We also agreed that team members who couldn't resolve a disagreement had the right to revisit the issue with the next level manager in either company.

Those types of principles, in some form or another, are pretty standard concepts within most successful companies, but we were creating a one-company model between two unique, distinct companies.

These principles, we decided, would guide us in four broad focus areas, which we identified as (1) simplifying the day-to-day business between the two companies, (2) developing an integrated approach to information management, (3) improving profitability for both companies, and (4) supporting store-tailored marketing efforts.

All four were important and were interconnected, but the one that probably stands out the most to me was improving the flow of information. This initially resulted in some pretty basic commitments, like the importance of sharing data between the two companies to answer key questions such as what products should be carried, how they should be priced, how they would be transported, how much inventory should be held, how products would be promoted, and how results would be tracked and measured.

The decision to be as transparent as possible would make it easy for people to see progress and support or recommend changes. And sharing data ensured we were coming to conclusions based on the same information. This was a fundamental bedrock to our success.

The commitment to sharing information also required an agreement to solve some technical problems that now seem archaic. It might sound crazy now, but in 1989 both companies had such thick firewalls in their information technology that email primarily served as an internal form of communication. In other words, members of the P&G-Walmart multifunctional team couldn't exchange an email with someone in the other company. Our entire P&G and Walmart business was done via fax machines. Walmart would fax purchase orders and we would fax them invoices. Can you imagine?!

Such simple, no-brainer issues were starting points that led to much more transformational changes in how retailers and suppliers share information, including the Retail Link system that allowed all suppliers, not just P&G, to see key data and product insights from Walmart.

Along with the operating principles and focus areas came initial objectives, measures, timelines, resource needs, and communication policies—all of which, to some degree or another, were developed during the second day of that two-day meeting.

We didn't solve every problem, but we went from what I considered an "intent to trust" to a framework that would allow both sides to demonstrate and build that trust. With that, we could look for better ways to do our existing work together, invent new ways of working together, and develop a relationship that would become systemic not just transactional.

We also established an accountability mechanism that was vital to maintaining momentum. For the next six months we ended every mirror team meeting with a review of our operating principles and evaluated how we were doing against them. Then when we identified any additional issues that were pain points, we resolved them before moving on.

Those issues continued to arise, but two important aspects of the team began to take root: One, our vastly different organizational cultures began to understand and learn from the other's strengths. And two, we aligned on a shared view of what we were doing and where we were going.

We didn't know the future, but we had a bike path that would take us there. We were building a bicycle made for two, however, so we still had to figure out how to peddle in unison without running into a ditch.

Notes

1. Sam Walton to John Smale, May 4, 1989 (author's personal collection).
2. Mike Graen, interview with the author, 2023.

CHAPTER 9

Structural Integrity

W e knew early on in our planning that we needed to make some radical changes to our P&G organizational structure for the one-company concept to work.

If all we wanted to do was put a team in place near Walmart's headquarters, we could have opened a sales office in Arkansas and gone on about our business. But we wanted to fundamentally disrupt how we did business together, and that required input and insights from a variety of functions in each of the organizations. That led to the idea that all the functions needed a seat at the table and then to the idea that members of corresponding functions with each company should have direct access to each other.

There were natural fits for this idea when it came to functions like finance, accounts payable, and logistics. But Walmart and P&G were different companies in different businesses. A company that creates, distributes, and markets consumer goods is not designed exactly the same as a business that operates retail stores and sells products to consumers.

This reality led to a series of new structures for the P&G teams that would serve Walmart and, later, all of our retail customers.

The onus was mostly on P&G to create these structures because we were the supplier and Walmart was our customer. Creating and executing a more strategic partnership relationship with Walmart was our full-time job. For the mirror team members from Walmart, it was additional work *on top of* their normal responsibilities. This meant we did prework on the front end that led to the work we did together, which led to us doing more work on our own that we then took back to the Walmart team for input and approval. And, of course, it meant we needed to structure our teams to work with Walmart's existing teams.

In the beginning, the most significant changes were the addition of an operations function for the P&G team, the combining of our sales and marketing functions, and the development of a customer service team.

These ideas originated from the interviews we had with Walmart associates in 1988. Then we took what I called a "peeling the onion" approach to learning and iterating until, layer by layer, we figured out what worked best for the relationship.

That's the way collaborative disruption happens. It doesn't follow a linear pattern; instead, one person's idea or observation leads to "So what?" and "What if?" questions, often from people in other functions. Contributions result in back-and-forth discussions, and previously unrealized solutions emerge that produce dramatically different ways of working.

Understanding Operations

When we started our assessment of how Walmart did business, we found out that they had a function called "operations" with layers that started in their home office and extended out to their stores.

The country was broken up into multiple regions, and each region had a vice president of operations who led a team of district managers who were responsible for the store managers in their district. Store managers weren't just merchants, they were effectively the CEOs of their stores and had profit responsibility.

We quickly realized how important and influential the operations function was within Walmart, and yet it was a function we knew almost nothing about. So we added an operations function within our Walmart Customer Team.

When I was announced as the team leader in January 1989, P&G also named Brad Simpson as the associate director of store operations, which probably shocked some folks since we didn't operate any stores. But Brad's role was to help the rest of our team understand the store operations of Walmart—what they did, why they did it, and how P&G fit within those operations. Once we had a person responsible for that, we were able to iterate our way to making it work.

One of Brad's first assignments was to spend a week in the field with a Walmart regional vice president of operations. So Brad left early one Monday morning on one of Walmart's corporate planes and didn't come back until late Thursday night.

He spent all four days with the Walmart vice president, who traveled from store to store talking to district managers and store managers about their operations. When Brad returned, he was able to describe in detail various aspects of Walmart's store operations and highlight opportunities he saw for us to contribute to increased sales and better in-store customer service.

Mixing It Up with Marketing

The marketing and sales functions within P&G both recruited new talent from the same pool of students at universities across the country, but those students started their careers at P&G in distinctly different ways.

In the P&G marketing department, new recruits were taught finance and general business skills, and they were involved in the basic running of the brands that made up the company's product portfolio. In the sales department, meanwhile, the newcomers learned persuasive selling techniques to achieve objectives that were assigned to their product division.

P&G's marketing executives tended to be the senior leaders of the company and were responsible for strategy, while leaders in the sales department were mainly considered as tactical resources.

When Lou Pritchett served as vice president of global sales, he looked for ways to bring marketing and sales together. The design team Lou created to research new ways of relating to customers included several people from marketing, because Lou knew they would have much more credibility when sharing our findings with the higher-level leaders in marketing.

The move gave the design team the much-needed perspective of the brand people who were actually making decisions for the company. And as the marketing folks learned about the dysfunctional relationships that existed between the sales department and their major customers, they immediately saw opportunities to improve their business and profitability by working in a different manner. So when we began to create the original Walmart team, we knew we needed to incorporate marketing into the structure.

Harry Campbell was a relatively young assistant brand manager in 1988 and, of course, he had ambitions of running his own brand for the company. But we somehow recruited him to join the team in a new role called group marketing manager that would combine his marketing skills with sales. And, as you might remember, he and his wife were the first team members to buy a house in Northwest Arkansas.

"I didn't have any idea what my job was, because I had never been in sales before," Harry recalled.[1]

Harry began to learn sales from veterans on our team like Bill Currie, the most senior member of the original sales team.

"I remember before I went for my first presentation to my buyer—the health and beauty aid buyer, Dennis Wagner, I believe was his name—I sat down with Bill Currie and asked for some tips," Harry told me. "'Nothing too fancy,' I said, 'but tell me what to do.' And he said, 'First of all, use as few words as you can and when you're done, you're done. Let them engage and fill the silence because they will. And don't ever forget you're Procter & Gamble. They need our products. But don't act like they do because they don't like that.'"[2]

Then Bill told him to never sell past the close.

"I had never heard that before," Harry said. "He was like, 'If they're already nodding their heads, they're giving you end caps, and you're getting a good order, just stop talking about it and start talking about the Razorbacks or something.'"[3]

Harry, meanwhile, brought a different approach to analytics and to putting together business propositions. And he wrote a monthly report that was broadly circulated to the marketing department in Cincinnati that described what he was learning and how it might make a difference in shaping the business strategies for a number of the brands he was very familiar with.

We also began to bring in advertising trainees—the fresh recruits to the marketing department who were required to do a six-month assignment somewhere in the United States with the sales department so they could gain exposure to P&G's customer base. The assignments were viewed as punishment because the trainees usually worked only with the smallest customers available. But we were able to incorporate them immediately into projects with a major customer.

These team members were young in the business, but they were the best and the brightest recruits. They brought a lot of enthusiasm to their work, and they had expertise, especially in analytics, from their first-year marketing training.

We gave them meaty projects to work on, and they communicated back to their respective marketing bosses on the value they were seeing from those projects. This ended up generating enthusiasm, and people from the marketing department started seeing the Walmart team as their preferred sales training assignment.

When the trainees returned to Cincinnati, of course, they maintained their relationships with the Walmart team. This helped them in their careers and in developing their business as they rose through the ranks to become brand managers. And it helped change the culture in marketing to have a greater appreciation for the power of an improved relationship with the customer.

Creating Continuous Replenishment

One of the most innovative aspects of Walmart's success was its approach to supply chain management. They revolutionized how distribution centers were located and operated, for instance, and their commitment to everyday low prices helped drive efficiencies throughout their system.

Product supply, of course, was a key aspect of P&G's operations, but we needed to meld what we knew and how we operated with what Walmart needed. So we created a customer service team that was responsible for developing supply efficiencies for the P&G brands in Walmart's stores.

Don Bechtel led this effort, and one of his first recruits in 1988 was Henry Ho, who at the time was working in the Central Distribution Office in Cincinnati.

"I was about half done with my MBA," Henry lamented, "and they said, 'Would you like to move and work with this little team down in Arkansas?' I'm like, 'Arkansas? Where's Arkansas?'"[4]

Henry eventually came to Arkansas and he's still there, but first he went to Dallas and became a tri-commuter—he made the circuit between Cincinnati, Dallas, and Arkansas.

The idea was to bring a team together in one location who all understood both P&G's and Walmart's ordering, delivery, and payment systems. This team, we believed, would collaborate with each other, cover for each other when needed, and produce better insights and services for the customer than individuals spread across the country with only one product division's focus.

So Henry moved to P&G's Southwest Distribution Office in Dallas to manage the team that was handling the Walmart business. After about eighteen months, he and most of the customer service representatives relocated to the new Fayetteville office.

This was a significant (and disruptive!) move since the five regional customer services offices across the country were being consolidated into a national office in Cincinnati, and it was important for us to have all of the folks managing the Walmart business in a single location.

Eventually, this group, in collaboration with Walmart, created and managed the TOM (Total Order Management) system. They were the equivalent of a 1-800 number for use by both companies in the coordination of the entire order, delivery, and payment process. No longer was it fragmented across multiple departments of Walmart and P&G.

The colocation enabled close cross-functional alignment, which in turn allowed us to give the customer service organization complete responsibility for TOM. Each customer service representative was responsible for all support (and results) from the time an order was generated until it was delivered and paid for. No more "up and down the daisy chain" communications between sales and other support organizations.

In turn, this led to significantly higher levels of customer focus, faster reaction and response times for problem resolution related to ordering issues, less rework, and a whole new level of trust, confidence, and collaboration between the two companies.

This was an outstanding example of a win-win for both companies, but, like many disruptive ideas, it got off to a rough start that illustrates the persistence and passion of our team.

As with any new system, there were some kinks during the development stage of the Continuous Replenishment Program (CRP). So there were many nights and weekends in early 1990 when the customer service team ensured the continuous flow of product to Walmart by doing whatever it took to fix and rekey orders into the system.

During those times, we would bring food in for the team to keep them going and to thank them for their hard work. It was an incredible sacrifice, especially for leaders like Sharon Minter (paper goods/diapers) and Karen Swofford (packaged soap) who managed high-turn categories, as well as for their families. Theresa Lewis was our utility player who eventually led that entire department as senior logistics operations before her retirement. Their heroic efforts helped role model for the team our "promises made, promises kept" mantra with the customer.

It was also during this period that Marianne Lingardo, the CRP leader in Cincinnati, recognized we needed someone in Arkansas full time to keep the system running smoothly. So she, along with her husband, agreed to move. As a bonus, her husband turned out to be a terrific short-stop on our company softball team.

Over the years, the customer service team has collaborated with their Walmart counterparts on everything from implementing higher-quality pallets, to coordinating with trucking companies on more efficient ways to schedule and deliver products, to managing deductions that occur if an invoice doesn't match what was delivered.

Invoice accuracy was a particularly important early win for this team because they solved a problem we at P&G initially didn't think existed. During a mirror team meeting, one of the Walmart members complained that as few as 15 percent of P&G invoices were paid as issued and with-out manual intervention to correct an accuracy issue. I found this odd, because our internal measurements told us we had 99 percent perfect orders.

I pulled out a $100 bill and put it on the table.

"I'll bet you a hundred bucks it's much closer to my number than it is to your number," I said.

They took the bet, and I agreed to pay a third party to spend three months recording and reviewing every P&G invoice to see how often it was payable and how often it required intervention.

I lost my bet.

But in the process, we learned the flaws in our system that were result-ing in the invoice inaccuracy, much of it having to do with differences in terminology or how we entered information that sometimes changed from the time orders were made, delivered, and invoiced.

"It boiled down to a pretty simple thing," Don Bechtel said. "They had prices for our items in their system that were different from the prices we had in our system. That's the easiest way to say it."[5]

Walmart, Don pointed out, paid based on the purchase order, not the invoice, and if their purchase order price was different from our invoice price, then there was an inaccuracy.

Don and Henry's team, along with Mike Graen's technology team, figured out not only what the problem was but how to track the informa-tion accurately. Prices were compared in each company's system when an order was placed, and discrepancies were resolved prior to shipment and billing.

The TOM system is a classic example of restructuring the way work gets done between a customer and supplier and the benefits that accrue to both organizations.

In this case, the important business process changes greatly simplified and consolidated the work and provided more ownership for the outcome. P&G initially added costs and reduced them for Walmart; however, the benefits for Walmart were huge in terms of cash flow since inventory turns on P&G products were significantly improved and in a short period of time.

For P&G, we more than recouped the initial cost increase to implement the process through better inventory management with our suppliers and more production efficiencies at our plants, as well as by getting better rates in transportation costs because the system was more predictable. Also, our common consumer was better served by improved in-stocks in the stores and fresher products. It was a classic win-win!

The concept of adding functions from Walmart and P&G continued to evolve as time went on, eventually including areas such as market research, packaging, legal, public relations, and international. And when Walmart opened or focused on a new store format (like neighborhood stores) or e-commerce, we added specific resources to match up with them.

In other words, once we had the basic structure in place, we could adapt it to the evolving needs of both businesses and, ultimately, to the benefit of consumers. It was a classic example of the whole equaling more than the sum of the parts.

Notes

1. Harry Campbell, interview with the author, 2023.
2. Campbell, interview.
3. Campbell, interview.
4. Henry Ho, interview with the author, 2023.
5. Don Bechtel, interview with the author, 2023.

Two in the Front

One of Mike Graen's first assignments when he moved to Arkansas was to answer what might seem like a pretty simple question: How much business does P&G do with Walmart?

Because P&G had been organized geographically and by brands, we could quickly tell you how much Tide we sold to a retail customer in Florida or how many cases of Pampers we sold to a retail customer in California. But we had no real-time database on our company-wide sales to any particular retailer. And the data we had took three weeks after the close of a month to access.

So Mike and his team spent about six weeks connecting databases to research how much product we were shipping to Walmart, then he created a report to share with Sam Walton and the other leaders of both companies.

The answer: ten million stat cases!

Sam Walton's response: "What the heck is a stat case?"

Statistical cases, as I briefly mentioned in an earlier chapter, were P&G's measurement for what we shipped to customers. It was a way of looking at our brands that allowed us to equalize the measurements for products we shipped like paper towels with cases for smaller products like toothpaste. Mike explained this to Sam, of course, but it really didn't matter.

"In the end," Mike recalled, "Walmart didn't care about stat cases or how much product we shipped to them."[1]

What mattered to Walmart was sales.

"I don't care what you ship me," I remember Sam telling us. "I care about how many dollars' worth of your products are sold through my registers and how much profit I make on the sales. And by the way, I don't make enough money on P&G."

"How much do you make?" we asked.

"I don't know," he said, "but it's not enough."

As disappointing as it was to discover we had just spent weeks researching data that didn't matter to our customer, there were some positives from all that work. It would become a powerful measurement for communicating within P&G, for instance, provided we were able to talk the retailer's language of sales in dollars. We also realized that this dilemma presented exactly the type of opportunity we were hoping for with the partnership.

"Mr. Sam, I have no idea how much of our products you sell," Mike said. "But I can tell you one thing: If we go get the data, we'll go figure it out."[2]

The secret to driving a two-company change, as we discovered, is for both parties to sit in the front seat, looking through the same windshield, with high-beam headlights on so we can clearly see the same road ahead.

Without shared data and transparency, it is like having two drivers looking through a peephole while driving in the dark with no headlights. But by openly sharing data from both companies, we could see further down the road and expand the windshield for a wider view of the opportunities.

Sharing data, of course, wasn't simple in those days. For one thing, retailers and suppliers had never shared their internal data with each other. Even with a signed confidentiality agreement, there was some natural resistance to the whole idea. For another, the technology wasn't in place to speed up the sharing of data and its analysis.

In fact, when Mike first went to Walmart and asked for sales data, the initial response was colder than the nose of the lead dog on an Iditarod sled race. Mike's counterpart in Walmart's IT department didn't see P&G as his supplier—he saw his suppliers as technology and software companies like AT&T, IBM, HP, and NCR. So he told Mike something like this: "I don't deal with P&G."

This type of reaction illustrates why support at the top of the organizations was so important.

"Mr. Sam sent me over here," Mike told his counterpart. "You want to tell him you won't give me the data?"[3]

With that, the on-ramp to the data opened up, but it didn't lead to an information superhighway. Back then, there wasn't an interstate from Fayetteville to Bentonville, just a mostly two-lane Highway 71.

"That was the information highway," joked Brian Barkocy, one of the members of Mike's team who began driving to Bentonville multiple times per week to load data from Walmart onto 3.5-inch floppy disks.[4] They would bring the disks back to our offices, download the data onto our computers, and mine it for insights about how our brands were selling in Walmart's stores.

One of the biggest initial realizations derived from the early data was that we needed to align on a shared view of success so we could make better decisions. As it turned out, we saw success in the large quantity of shipments we made to Walmart—look at all those stat cases! Walmart, meanwhile, saw success when it sold products at an everyday low price and still made a profit, and by that measure its relationship with P&G was a flop.

Walmart sold most P&G products for less than its competitors, which was great for consumers but not good for Walmart's bottom line. In fact, Walmart was losing money on many of our brands and on its overall business with P&G. It stocked our brands because they were popular with shoppers. Those shoppers would show up for a great deal on Tide, for instance, but fill their baskets with other items that were more profitable to Walmart.

Since many of our brands were essentially loss leaders, Walmart had little incentive to increase its sales on those P&G products. Selling more only turbo-charged Walmart's losses.

Once we both were in the front seat together looking at the same data and freshly aligned on a better destination, we could develop plans that improved Walmart's margins on our products, in some cases by just a little and in others by a great deal. By 1991—just three years after we began forming the customer service team—Walmart had nearly tripled its sales of P&G products and its profits on P&G sales improved by around $40 million.

The emphasis on mining and sharing data also contributed to one of the most disruptive innovations in the history of the retail industry: Retail Link. Walmart initiated the project, putting together a committee that included their folks, some people from our team such as Mike, experts from the University of Arkansas, and representatives of other suppliers who weren't P&G competitors.

The combined forces in this collaborative disruption spent a couple of years developing a free platform that was launched in 1992 and was used until 2024 when it was replaced with Walmart Luminate.

For more than thirty years, Retail Link allowed Walmart's suppliers to access the retailer's daily sales data so they can analyze and improve their business. Suppliers could see things like how much of your product you sold at each store, how much you sold it for, how much Walmart made on it, how much inventory there is at that store, what promotions were in play, and what options you have for replenishing the product.

With a large supplier like P&G, you're talking about thousands of different items that are sold at thousands of different stores, so that's a ton of data. Retail Link provided an artificial intelligence model—one of the early applications of AI, in fact—that allowed us to look over that data in the morning and immediately identify the things we needed to fix or keep an eye on.

"Basically, there was a problem and we solved the problem by looking at the data," Mike told me. "We fixed the problem and then Walmart said, 'I want to reapply it to my other suppliers.' That is the Retail Link story."[5]

Taking Stock

In an attempt to connect our original team to Walmart's business, I decided in 1990 to give all of our team members one share of Walmart stock.

It was mainly symbolic, but it also came with the advantage of gaining us access to Walmart's shareholder's meetings. On the other hand, it was against P&G's policy, so we had to leap through several hoops with our chief legal officer and get approval from our CEO to purchase one share for each team member. It became even more complicated when the shares split before I could get the team their certificates. We had approval for one share, but now everyone had two.

Two shares weren't much, and most of the team framed a paper copy of their shares and displayed it in their offices, much to the delight of our frequent visitor from Walmart. Those shares, of course, continued to grow like weeds as shares in Walmart continued to split. Bill Toler, who was instrumental in getting our team up and running and eventually retired from P&G as a global vice president, told me he still has his original framed certificate hanging on a wall in his home in Colorado. Those two shares are now 36 shares.

Searching for Fresh Perspectives

One of the unique ways we worked to ensure Walmart and P&G were sharing the front seat and looking through the same windshield at shared opportunities was to listen to sources who weren't even part of the mirror team.

That might sound counterintuitive, but we recognized that we all have limits to our knowledge and blind spots in our understanding. So we wanted to learn everything we could that was relevant to our relationship and then share it with each other as we drove down the road.

For instance, around 1992 I stumbled onto the value of listening to what the two companies were telling their investors.

I asked someone in P&G's investor relations division to review Walmart's annual report and give me his professional take on the retailer's goals and commitments. And not only did he give me his perspective but he also told me that every year big companies like P&G and Walmart would hold meetings in New York just for analysts.

What a great opportunity, I thought, *to glean insights about our customer.*

I wound up attending Walmart's analyst day in New York every year from that point until I retired. I listened to the Walmart presentation and the question-and-answer session, and on two occasions a Walmart presenter called on me to offer an opinion as a key supplier.

These meetings gave me great insights that shaped our team's focus, as well as our subsequent discussions with Walmart's senior officers. And because I was the only supplier representative there, it reinforced my credibility within both P&G and Walmart.

I also asked my contact on the P&G investor relations team to provide a recap after the P&G investor day so I'd know the specific promises that were made and any other issues that would likely come up in the future.

Again, this sharpened our focus as a team and made for much better communication within P&G because we made decisions and shared information with a more holistic understanding of both companies.

Attending Walmart's Saturday meetings, going on store visits with Walmart associates, and holding joint planning sessions in Cincinnati

with Walmart associates were other ways we gathered insights that
helped build trust and ensured we built a shared view of the future.

When Walmart expanded internationally, I even went to every first
store opening they had in a new global market. I would be the only corporate supplier representative there, which added to our credibility with
their senior executives and allowed me to foster relationships between
our leaders in those markets and their Walmart counterparts.

Aligning on Business

A monumental difference in our new way of working with Walmart was
that we no longer were approaching them as a sales team but as business partners, and that meant we had to adjust our understanding and
approach because the typical salesperson had very little understanding
of how business was done or the concerns of senior executives.

Later in my career I began explaining this transition with a hypothetical story involving former Walmart CEO David Glass.

Let's pretend David and I are having a conversation and he says, "Tom,
tell me what you do with your money internationally overnight."

I think it is a personal question about my international travel best practices, so I tell him that I take half of my money and put it in my shoe and
then put socks in the shoe so the money can't be seen. Then I put the
other half in my pillowcase so that I'm sleeping on it.

David looks at me like I'm from Jupiter, and it's only later that I realize
he was posing a business question and I had no clue what he was asking
me about.

My goal, and by extension our team's goal, was to understand every
level of Walmart's business so that we were in the front seat together
looking out the same window at the same view and helping each other
get where we both wanted to go.

One way we gained this type of alignment was by spending time with
our Walmart counterparts inside their organization and inviting them
into ours.

For instance, we took trips together to Cincinnati, where they were
able to see our R&D facilities, listen to how we handled the consumer
phone calls on our 1-800 lines, see our manufacturing facilities, and hear
presentations from our marketing groups, all of which helped them bet-

ter understand how a consumer product company works and, specifically, how it worked at P&G.

We also then took field trips with them and their leadership to stores and distribution centers around the country. We saw firsthand how products progressed from an order all the way to the cash register, which helped us understand the dynamics of retailing and how they managed in different markets compared with their competitors.

Our objective was to design processes with them at all levels that were transparent and beneficial to both companies, as well as to consumers. These collaborations disrupted the old way of doing things because P&G brands and categories representatives now would develop plans for expanding entire categories of sales. Rather than just focusing on P&G brands, we focused on helping both companies improve their market shares.

We worked together on areas like inventory turns, cash flow, and return on investment, which was atypical for retail customer-supplier relationships in those days.

We shared a lot of our proprietary information on brands, categories, and consumer data—things like purchase frequencies in various categories and regional and ethnic differences that could be applied to their store locations.

They shared data and learnings as well, and most importantly, the data and insights we shared were actionable within our relationship. This allowed us to get in the front seat together and chart a path to our shared success.

We even went so far as to order forty-five feet of the exact same shelving that Walmart used in their stores to create a "layout room" in our office. This allowed us to replicate a process that Walmart used in their layout room to make their annual shelf space and assortment changes by category.

We were able to combine their data and our data to create the optimal shelf and distribution arrangements for different demographics, geographies, and store sizes. We would then take pictures and provide details to our Walmart counterparts as recommendations that, if accepted, made their life easier. And if it needed some minor tweaks, it still was a time saver that came with fact-based rationale.

When this process was combined with our rolling eighteen-month planning cycle, we were able to have an agreed-on in-store shelf plan for new item launches that would happen between the annual reviews. This was a big deal for both companies, and it illustrates how shared vision, beliefs, passions, courage, persistence, humility, and gratitude were operationalized in very real ways to disrupt the old ways of doing retail.

The Business Process

The process we used during that initial trip to Bentonville became a go-to approach for achieving breakthrough results that others did not think were possible.

First, we identified the opportunities we thought were promising or the problems that needed to be fixed. In each case we determined what the result would be if we were successful, and we called that the "size of the prize."

We then developed a vision of what success would look like, or what Stephen R. Covey would describe as beginning with the end in mind.

From the vision, we would make a joint determination to bring the vision to life. This was the decision stage of the process, and it ensured alignment and a willingness to commit the time, energy, and resources needed to make it happen.

Our next step was to share the idea or problem with each function so we could identify what each business unit would require, at what time, and in what sequence.

From that input we built and implemented a prototype that allowed us to learn quickly and inexpensively to validate whether the idea was as worthwhile as we thought and to ensure we understood the true cost relative to the "size of the prize."

From there, we adjusted based on the results so that we were able to actually deliver what we had identified in the vision. At Walmart, they called this process "the correction of errors."

Then we would expand the idea and continue to monitor the business results to ensure it was delivering on the "size of the prize" that we had used to determine the amount of investment we would make into the idea.

Assuming the results were what we had planned, we would celebrate our success. If the results were not what we had hoped, we would reassess to determine whether the idea was just not as powerful as we thought or if we had made a mistake in the execution that could be rectified with another change.

Once we had a successful execution, we would try to make that more of a standard operating process within P&G and in Walmart. Within P&G, we would look to try the idea across different brands and in different categories or in other situations that were similar. Walmart would look to achieve benefits from executing the idea more broadly within their company.

Notes

1. Mike Graen, interview with the author, 2023.
2. Graen, interview.
3. Graen, interview.
4. Brian Barkocy, interview with the author, 2023.
5. Graen, interview.

CHAPTER 11

Comparative Cultures

When it came right down to it, all the grand plans, operating principles, and processes in the world wouldn't matter if the relationships between the people directly involved in this new way of doing business didn't thrive.

The good news was that for all our many differences, Walmart and P&G shared some important common ground.

There's a reason Walmart and P&G both ended up as examples of "visionary companies" in *Built to Last*, Jim Collins and Jerry I. Porras's classic book on what it takes to sustain excellence in business over a long period of time. The two companies, for instance, shared common values (like high integrity), common strategies (like their shared commitment to the new partnership), and common incentives for motivating our teams (like profit sharing for all employees).

In fact, when we charted the basic beliefs expressed by P&G and compared them with those expressed by Walmart, there were some remarkable correlations:

P&G	Walmart
Consumer is at the heart of all we do	Customer is always No. 1
The best people	Ordinary people producing extraordinary results
Trusted leadership brands	"Trust" is Walmart's leadership brand
Employee ownership	Associate ownership
Do the right thing	Do the right thing
Relentless quest to be the best	Strive for excellence
Improve the lives of the world's consumers	Lower the worldwide cost of living— Always Low Prices

Sam Walton summarized Walmart's core value in what he called the company's four basic beliefs: service to the customer, respect for the individual, strive for excellence, and act with integrity. Mike Graen, our first functional leader for information technology, and I were discussing these values not long ago, and he said, "It's especially clear from my experience that those were values of the P&G Walmart team."[1] I couldn't agree more.

The differences in our cultures created some very real challenges, but the shared foundation based on those basic beliefs allowed us to not only work through the challenges but learn from each other and improve.

As the saying goes, culture eats strategy for breakfast, and the only way we could get to the strategy was by making culture—or, in this case, cultures—a high priority.

There really were four cultures involved in the early stages of the partnership: those of P&G, Walmart, the mirror team, and P&G's Walmart team. The mirror team, however, was more short-lived. Its culture is best understood by looking at the agreed operating principles and the initial goals and objectives that were outlined in chapter 8. That team got the partnership up and rolling, then became less of a formal entity as the one-company collaboration model became broader and more ingrained in both companies.

P&G's Walmart team, however, was birthed from the cultures of the two corporate companies and then grew into something uniquely its own. Perhaps the best way to understand the offspring, then, is to look more closely at the cultures of its parents.

The Walmart Way

Walmart is known for its commitment to its customers. Sam Walton saw this as the key to success for any company. He made it a top priority from the beginning and expressed the idea often and in many ways.

For instance:

- "There is only one boss. The customer. And he can fire everybody in the company from the chairman on down, simply by spending his money somewhere else."[2]
- "Walmart's future will depend on how well you take care of each of your customers. A day at a time. A customer at a time. A store at a time."[3]

- "Business is a competitive endeavor, and job security lasts only as long as the customer is satisfied. Nobody owes anybody else a living."[4]

This commitment has been lived out by associates in a variety of ways over the years, starting, of course, with Walmart's relentless drive to provide everyday low prices. They believe this philosophy improves the standard of living for their customers because it allows them to make their paychecks go further.

To keep prices consistently low for their customers, they have to keep expenses low throughout the company. As Walton said, "Every time Wal-Mart spends one dollar foolishly, it comes right out of our customers' pockets."[5]

The value of every dollar was so ingrained in their culture when our partnership began that next to every copy machine in the home office was a pallet of shredded paper with a sign on it that said, "Do you really need to make that many copies?"

Each manager in the company also had their own profit and loss statements (P&Ls), so they were accountable to help make the low-cost goal a reality. This led to actions that we often saw in our work with Walmart's leaders. When they traveled, they didn't stay at the most expensive hotels and they shared rooms. I actually teased them by saying they believed any hotels with rooms that opened to an interior hall rather than to a parking lot were considered five-star establishments.

They also had a policy that they could not charge alcohol on the company when traveling, so many of them had one credit card to pay for their meals and a personal card if they decided they wanted an alcoholic drink.

Brad Simpson, our first operations manager, spent a week traveling with a Walmart regional vice president early in the development of our team. When he turned in his expenses, there was a receipt for a fifth of Jack Daniel's whiskey.

"Brad, I'm happy if you have a drink or two on the company," I said, "but don't you think this is a bit excessive?"

He explained that he and his Walmart counterpart had shared a room and that Walmart paid for it. Since his colleague couldn't write off alcohol, Brad figured the least he could do was pay for their drinks for the week. It was hard to argue that logic, so I signed off on the expense report.

Keeping prices (and expenses) low wasn't the only way Walmart demonstrated a culture that valued the customer. For instance, Walmart also has always had a very liberal return policy—if you don't like it, bring it back for a refund.

Suppliers haven't always cared for this policy because most returned items can't be resold. They end up in a damaged goods warehouse and the manufacturer or supplier has to give Walmart credit. But customers love the return policy, sometimes too much. When we first started our partnership, we heard stories about a few customers going so far as to buy a lawnmower at the start of the summer and return it in early fall.

Most customers, of course, didn't take such a blatant advantage of a return policy; instead, their loyalty increased because they knew they could always return something if they had a legitimate reason.

Walmart also put the customer first by sending home office associates to stores to help during busy seasons like around Thanksgiving or Christmas or by encouraging store associates to go the extra mile to help a customer in need, which is why you might see one helping a customer change a flat tire in the parking lot.

The culture of Walmart wasn't just about serving the customer, though. For instance, the company is overtly patriotic. It has long had an aggressive approach to hiring veterans, and to my knowledge no honorably discharged veteran who applied for a job with Walmart has ever been turned down.

Sam Walton also started his Made in America campaign as a means of supporting other businesses across the country. Walmart would make unusually long purchase agreements so that newer companies could get favorable bank loans they needed to meet production timelines. And in some cases Walmart loaned suppliers money to help them build facilities they needed to produce American-made products.

Walmart's culture also was, and as far as I know still is, very transparent and very empowered by role. You could see how that played out in their Saturday morning meetings, which all the managers in their home office attended.

The executives sat at the front of the auditorium facing the other attendees, and together they reviewed their business in great detail, so the home office associates were extremely well informed about what was going on in the company. They knew the issues Walmart faced. They knew where they were seeing success. And they knew where action had to be taken.

I was amazed at how fast they went from idea to action. They say retail is detail, and that certainly was the case with Walmart. At the end of those meetings, the operation's regional managers held conference calls with their district managers to communicate new action items. Then the district managers would conduct conference calls with their store managers. As a result, ideas and actions agreed on at the Saturday morning meeting were typically implemented by the next day.

When I wasn't on vacation, I attended every Saturday morning meeting for the first four or five years that I was there, and it was an amazing experience. Not only did I learn a great deal about the retail industry and about our key customer, but it was a great time for me to touch base with fifteen to twenty associates whom I needed to talk to for three to five minutes. We wouldn't have had an in-person meeting just for that subject, but I was able to keep the communication lines open.

I also saw their senior leadership in action. At the end of each meeting, Sam Walton, David Glass, or Don Soderquist would give a five- to ten-minute talk. It could be on any topic, from patriotism to community service to leadership to whatever, but it was always well done and inspirational, and it helped you grow personally and professionally.

Their senior leaders came across very much as real people. They did not partake of the traditional executive trappings when it came to things like the size of their offices and special parking places, and they made a point to speak to associates in stores, the home office cafeteria (where they ate with everyone else), or wherever else they came together.

And while there was a lot of self-deprecating humor at the Saturday morning meetings as the executives poked fun at each other and themselves, they also challenged each other and their associates. There was a high degree of accountability. You needed to know your business from the previous week because you could easily get called on at any point in the meeting. Most associates were at their desks an hour before the meeting started to review their P&Ls for the week that ended the night before. That was also a sign of the strength of their information systems.

Dealing with Drawbacks

Walmart's culture also had some drawbacks. They had a ready-fire-aim mentality, for instance, so their associates were empowered to make decisions, but they often made them without sufficient data or a full perspective. They made many decisions that they fully believed were in the best interest of Walmart but that in fact weren't, simply because they lacked a full picture of the decision's impact.

As you might expect, these decisions frequently caused problems for suppliers like P&G, but it was very difficult to get people to change their minds.

Additionally, they were so focused on everyday low prices that they tended to think of every product as a commodity and, therefore, the only difference was the price. I remember having conversations with them about Tide, our premium laundry detergent. They thought it was too expensive compared with a private-label brand. So my challenge was to reframe the issue.

For the sake of argument, I'd say, let's agree that each bottle does fifty loads of laundry. So that means Tide costs 50 cents a load and the private-label brand costs just 25 cents a load. But let's keep in mind that the customer has around $200 to $300 worth of clothes in each load. And those clothes will wear out faster, won't smell as fresh, and won't look as nice when washing with the budget brand. Is it really worth taking that risk with your clothes to save a quarter?

Besides, I'd say, if Tide did not justify the premium price, people wouldn't buy it. It's the market leader, so a lot of people must see the value in paying extra for cleaner, better-cared-for clothes.

We had this type of conversation often over the years. Later in the relationship, for instance, we made this point with a unique demonstration for Doug Degn, a senior Walmart executive who would retire as an executive vice president. We showed him two white golf-type shirts that each had been washed ten times, one with Tide and the other with a private-label brand. Predictably, Tide won.

We had to work against their culture to help them understand how the value of product performance difference earned the premium price. But we also had to work within, and sometimes against, our own corporate culture.

Marching in Step with P&G

P&G's culture, meanwhile, was very formal and hierarchical. Most of the senior leadership were World War II veterans, so the company was in many ways organized on a military model of command and control.

For example, the six sections within the sales organization formed a unit. Three units formed a district. Six districts formed a division. Five divisions formed a product division. And each product division had a great deal of autonomy to set their direction and operate the way they thought was best for them.

Nothing required these divisions to have the same policies with customers, however, and they often didn't. This was very confusing, complicated, and irritating to our customers since to them, each product division was P&G.

We also had a policy of promoting from within. You joined the company at an entry level, and everybody above you had held the same role you now had. As you moved up, your boss always had the role you were moving into.

And P&G was very selective in its hiring, taking only the best of the best college graduates and typically from a core group of universities. If you looked at the number of job applicants and the number of hires, we figured it was more difficult to get a job at P&G than to get into Harvard Business School.

In those days, the P&G workforce was larger than Walmart's, and by the late 1970s we already operated globally. So one of the strengths of our culture was that we had more diversity in our ranks than typically found in corporate America at that time.

Arkansas was pretty homogeneous, especially in the business community. But our leadership team included women, African Americans, and people of a variety of faith backgrounds. They were experts in their roles, but they also helped us see perspectives where we would otherwise have blind spots.

In fact, we had team members from more than twelve countries, and the two highest-ranking African American members of any customer business development team, Kim Robinson and Barron Witherspoon, worked with us. Both eventually became vice presidents at P&G, and while on our team they contributed enormously to the business, the community, and the University of Arkansas.

The corporate world seems to have picked up on the value of diverse teams in the last decade or so, and to that I'd say, "Welcome to the soup party!" The way we always saw it, the issue was not to create a puree but to make a great soup with as many vegetables as possible. When it came together with the right seasonings, the flavor was incredible.

P&G's key levers for success, meanwhile, also shaped our culture. These primarily involved R&D and marketing, which were part of each product division. All the other functions were important, but they tended to be more tactical to support those two.

In the same way that Walmart's focus on the customer translated into everyday low prices, our focus on the customer played out in our obsession with meeting our consumers' needs through our investments in R&D and marketing.

We had a very talented group of market researchers who would find out what consumers needed and where those needs weren't being met in our offerings. P&G was known for product innovations and creating new categories such as fabric softeners, disposable diapers, and stackable potato chips.

We did extensive product testing before taking a product to the market. We also were one of the first companies to have 1-800 numbers on all of our packaging so consumers could call with any issues—questions about a product's instructions, for instance, or problems with how the product performed. And P&G was very quick to take action to resolve those consumer issues.

Walmart was impressed by the way we provided consumers with product excellence. It wasn't something they had appreciated about products like ours, but it paralleled the extra miles they would go to exceed their customers' expectations.

The more Walmart's understanding of our product testing and product quality grew, the more it helped when we introduced new items. Walmart knew how thoroughly the new products had been researched and tested, so we didn't have long negotiations over whether they would stock the product. Because they knew we weren't going to come out with something that wasn't an excellent product, we could spend our time together figuring out how to sell more of the product when it launched.

This benefited both companies. We benefited from the sales, of course. And Walmart benefited because retailers that aggressively support a new product early in its life cycle typically end up with a larger long-term market share than their competitors.

P&G's focus on innovation wasn't limited to products. From a marketing perspective, we were storytellers; we didn't just sell soap. We created soap operas. We also introduced major new brands with house-to-house sampling, where we actually hung samples, such as detergent, on consumers' doors across the country.

In the sales organization, however, the P&G culture was less about innovation and more about supporting the product divisions in whatever ways they deemed necessary to influence our retail customers. Therefore, we seldom focused on the impact what we were asking might have on the customers' systems. In fact, I used to joke that the first thing we did when we hired someone in sales at P&G was cut off their ears so they could broadcast but couldn't listen.

As a company, we were very analytical. While Walmart was ready-fire-aim, we were ready, aim, aim again, change the scope, aim one more time, then fire. Being very deliberate is good in many respects because the closer you get to the target, the more likely you are to hit a bullseye.

Another feature of our culture was that there wasn't much autonomy in most of the lower-level jobs. You had some responsibility and decision making, but it was small in relation to the impact of your role.

Information was given out on a need-to-know basis, and there was not much openness and transparency with the senior executives, who had their own floor of the building and special elevators that zipped them directly from their reserved parking spots to their big offices. If you were called up there, it was always a very formal and intimidating session.

All of the product divisions had a floor in the building, and their senior executives had the corner offices. Every time you got promoted, you got a bigger office.

Common Ground

Walmart's culture wasn't necessarily better than P&G's, nor was P&G's necessarily better than Walmart's. In some cases, we could learn from them, in some cases they could learn from us, and in some cases we simply needed to be different because we were different companies with different histories and different rationales for how we operated.

To work together effectively, however, we needed to understand the cultural differences and how and why they resulted in different approaches to the way we did business. Here's a snapshot of how the two companies operated differently in the formative years:

P&G	Walmart
Perfection before speed	Speed before perfection.
Analyze deeply to avoid mistakes	Broad and fast testing and use of correction of errors in expansion
Product portfolio is targeted to a range of best and some better products	Offer good-better-best product range
Geographic and product line matrix decision-making process	Both top-down and bottom-up decision making
Use category by country P&Ls with limited visibility in the organization	Use store P&Ls with multiple aggregations and high visibility within the organization
Use cost averages in decision making	Use absolute cost in decision making

In many ways, the long-term success of the one-company model hinged on our correctly answering the following question: How well would P&G's Walmart team develop a unique culture of its own that honored the cultures and best practices of both Walmart and P&G?

Notes

1. Mike Graen, interview with the author, 2023.
2. "The Story of the Walmart Spark," Walmart Digital Museum, accessed April 16, 2024, https://www.walmartmuseum.com/content/walmartmuseum/en_us/timeline/decades/2000/artifact/3932.html.
3. "Story of the Walmart Spark."
4. Sam Walton, *Sam Walton: Made in America* (New York: Random House, 2012), Kindle edition, 234.
5. Walton, *Sam Walton: Made in America*, 12.

1989 Steering Team, pictured are Brad Simpson, Mike Graen, Don Bechtel (first row), Bill Toler, Tom Muccio, Kathy Blair (second row). *Image courtesy of Mike Graen.*

The entire Walmart P&G Customer Team in 1990. *Image courtesy of Mike Graen.*

The Walmart P&G Customer Team grew exponentially thanks to our successful efforts. This image is only of our US team; we had the same size team around the globe in countries where Walmart operates. *Image courtesy of Mike Graen.*

Beefo lived outside the first P&G office building in Fayetteville. We would say it was the only P&G office where the BS was outside the office. *Image courtesy of the author.*

Signed Hog hats were the official parting gift for those leaving our team. *Image courtesy of Jesse Edelman.*

Years later, Jesse Edelman's most prized business possessions are the awards and memorabilia from his time on the team. *Image courtesy of Jesse Edelman.*

The values wall at ArchPoint demonstrates that the principles our P&G team put forth live on today within the companies that former team members now lead. *Image courtesy of Jesse Edelman.*

The practice of recognizing outstanding team members still thrives in the companies led by former team members. *Image courtesy of Jesse Edelman.*

Harry Campbell still has the one share of Walmart stock that I gave to each team member in 1990. Now worth 37.5 shares! *Image courtesy of Harry Campbell.*

It was important that everyone signed off—literally—on the high standards set in our team's operating principles. *Image courtesy of Jesse Edelman.*

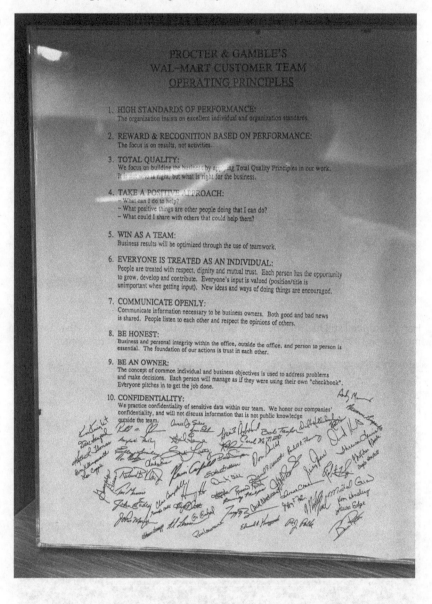

PROCTER & GAMBLE'S
WAL-MART CUSTOMER TEAM
OPERATING PRINCIPLES

1. HIGH STANDARDS OF PERFORMANCE:
The organization insists on excellent individual and organization standards.

2. REWARD & RECOGNITION BASED ON PERFORMANCE:
The focus is on results, not activities.

3. TOTAL QUALITY:
We focus on building the business by applying Total Quality Principles in our work.
It is not who is right, but what is right for the business.

4. TAKE A POSITIVE APPROACH:
– What can I do to help?
– What positive things are other people doing that I can do?
– What could I share with others that could help them?

5. WIN AS A TEAM:
Business results will be optimized through the use of teamwork.

6. EVERYONE IS TREATED AS AN INDIVIDUAL:
People are treated with respect, dignity and mutual trust. Each person has the opportunity
to grow, develop and contribute. Everyone's input is valued (position/title is
unimportant when getting input). New ideas and ways of doing things are encouraged.

7. COMMUNICATE OPENLY:
Communicate information necessary to be business owners. Both good and bad news
is shared. People listen to each other and respect the opinions of others.

8. BE HONEST:
Business and personal integrity within the office, outside the office, and person to person is
essential. The foundation of our actions is trust in each other.

9. BE AN OWNER:
The concept of common individual and business objectives is used to address problems
and make decisions. Each person will manage as if they were using their own "checkbook".
Everyone pitches in to get the job done.

10. CONFIDENTIALITY:
We practice confidentiality of sensitive data within our team. We honor our companies'
confidentiality, and will not discuss information that is not public knowledge
outside the team.

Another proud moment: the 1991 purchase order that put P&G over one billion dollars in sales for that fiscal year. *Image courtesy of Harry Campbell.*

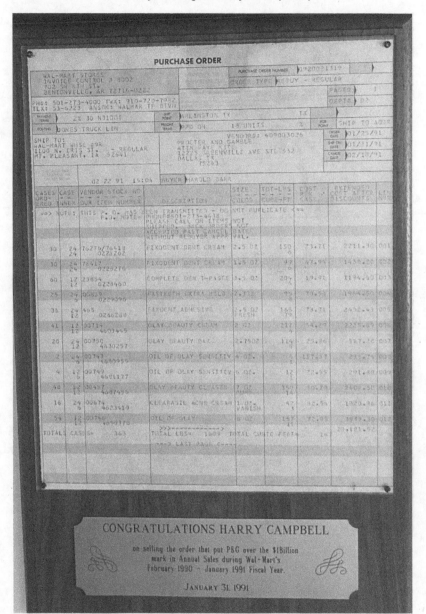

Lou Pritchett, Barbara Pritchett, Helen Walton, and Sam Walton on a Spring River float trip. *Image courtesy of Lou Pritchett.*

Mr. Sam canoeing on the Spring River, the place where it all started. *Image courtesy of Lou Pritchett.*

H. Lee Scott served as CEO of Walmart from 2000–2009. He was a strong supporter of our shopper marketing work. *Image courtesy of Mike Graen.*

A. G. Lafley, a member of the executive steering team to reenvision P&G's relationship with Walmart, later served as CEO of P&G from 2000–2010 and 2013–2015. *Image courtesy of Mike Graen.*

H. Lee Scott Sr. has been CEO of Walmart from 2000-2009. He was a strong supporter of our shopper marketing work. Image courtesy of Mike Green.

A.G. Lafley, a member of the executive steering team in recognition P&G's relationship with Walmart, later served as CEO twice from 2000-2010 and 2013-2015 (image courtesy of Mike Green.)

CHAPTER 12

The Path of the Pathfinders

Lou Pritchett, who played such a crucial role in the genesis of the Walmart-P&G relationship, retired on May 30, 1989, and he gave a brief farewell speech that covered eight things he had learned during his time with P&G.

It was all good advice, but one part seemed specifically relevant to me and for our team in Arkansas.

"I've learned that the real value to our company in the '90s will not be managers who teach people to execute," Lou said. "It will be the leaders who teach people to *dream*. And we must make room for dreamers and create an environment where the price our people pay to effect change is not so painful that few people are willing or able to pay it. Because an *idea* is one thousand times more powerful than a *fact*, and our success will require that we value ideas in the future more than we've valued facts in the past."[1]

P&G's culture, like all cultures, linked us to the past, Lou pointed out. The challenge for those who remained at the company, he said, was to create the future. And that mantra became central to our team's identity. It was our culture. It was our brand. We arrived as pioneers, but we became pathfinders.

Lou, who went on to a successful second career as a consultant and corporate speaker, labeled our team the "pathfinders" during a lunch for our new members on his final day at P&G. And Mike Milligan, who followed Lou as vice president of sales, ran with that moniker in September 1989 when we gathered at the Queen City Club in Cincinnati for a customer business development lunch.

Almost everyone on our new team was there, and Mike delivered some remarks about how we were doing as a company and about his views on our move to a multifunctional customer team with Walmart. Mike shared his notes with me, so I can paraphrase what he said pretty accurately.

"The future of the sales restructure—or, to put it a better way, the strategic alliance and close working cooperation with our customers as an integral part of our corporate strategy—is being led by you," he told us. "You are the pathfinders who lead the way."[2]

The pathfinder analogy came from the foreword of *The Longest Day,* a book by Cornelius Ryan that tells the story of D-Day during World War II. Obviously, our contributions don't hold a candle to those of the soldiers who stormed the beaches of Normandy, many giving their lives for our freedom. Lou's brother was killed in action on Utah Beach, so he was related to a true pathfinder. Lou and Mike were just drawing a parallel about how we were forging important new paths in uncertain terrains.

"From my perspective," Mike said, "our company has the right people as its pathfinders."[3]

In our shared journey from pioneers to pathfinders, we had to band together in a supportive culture that would allow us to tap into the power of new ideas, and that's exactly what happened. This culture had several important characteristics, and I believe any team leading a collaborative change or taking a one-company approach would do well to emulate them.

Our Unique Identity

For starters, our culture embraced the mission, vision, and values of Walmart and P&G.

The original Walmart-P&G mirror team laid the groundwork for this by developing a joint mission statement that we carefully crafted so that none of our members felt anything in it contradicted the guiding beliefs of either company.

The mirror team eventually went away, with the P&G leadership team engaging more strategically with the senior management of Walmart, first at the home office in Bentonville and later, as Walmart expanded globally, with their leaders around the world.

The P&G customer service team, meanwhile, blossomed within a culture that honored Walmart and P&G but that was unique to a pathfinder spirit. We were an experimental team full of mavericks, mixing our ideas with the inevitable influences of Walmart to create new ways of doing business.

I see this in much the same way I see the Christian church. As a follower of Jesus, I have visited congregations around the world that worship in very different ways from our churches in America, but our core beliefs are the same. P&G's outpost in Arkansas had different expressions of the company's corporate culture, but our basic beliefs remained true and consistent with those of anyone in the world who worked for the company.

The best example of how this played out involved our offices in Fayetteville, which were much smaller than those in Cincinnati, especially for the more senior leaders. In fact, all of our offices were the same size and the corner offices were used as conference rooms. The only reserved parking places were for our Walmart team members who visited for meetings, which sent a very powerful signal (to them and to our team) about how we viewed them.

None of that went against the mission, vision, and values of P&G, but it made sense for how we would do business, especially as a team working with Walmart.

As leaders, we wanted to create a brand identity that shaped how everyone thought about our team. Walmart and P&G already were dominant brands, so we had that as a solid foundation. We built on those reputations and added our own unique twists.

We were intentionally aspirational, so we set high expectations and built a culture that encouraged and rewarded new ideas and new ways of working. We wanted to reinvent ourselves as the world around us changed, so consistent high achievement and constant relevance were a standard from the start.

The culture had the feel of a successful sports team that was constantly focused on winning as a team and improving our performance through a disciplined approach and hard work. The expectation was that at the end of every day your uniform should be dirty.

There was great support and cheering for each other, and no one demonstrated that more than Mike Russell, who was on the team from 1992 to 2017. I gave him the title of president of the "ain't no mountain high enough that we can't climb it" club.

In tough times, Mike would come to my office and say, "Put me in, coach, I'm ready to play." At our Monday morning huddle meetings, he frequently reminded folks, "We are playing for the best team, up against the toughest competition, and with the largest customer in the world." He would then shout out, "Remember, every play counts!"

That type of attitude motivated the team to win the first company-wide Chairman's Club Award for excellence and business contribution, which we repeatedly won in future years, as well as walking away with many of the individual awards by team members.

It also helped that we were committed to high levels of transparency and accountability, which was in keeping with the "promises made, promises kept" motto.

We held each other accountable not only to goals but in how we treated each other. For this, I drew from a principle I learned in Matthew 18:15–17 of the Bible, which basically says if someone sins against you then you should first talk to that person. If you can't resolve it, then you bring in one or two other people, and if that doesn't work, then you take it to the church for the appropriate resolution. In the same way, we challenged everyone to do all they could to resolve their disputes between each other before elevating the issue to a supervisor.

If someone came to me with a complaint about another employee, my standard response was, "What did they say to you when you brought this up with them?" If they hadn't done that, then I sent them away to do it.

Some of our commitment to accountability came directly from what I learned from Sam Walton. If you operated on "Sam's time," for instance, you arrived thirty minutes before a meeting was scheduled to begin or you were late. Thus, the parking lots were full on Saturday mornings for their meetings at least a half hour before the meetings began.

We picked up on the spirit of that idea and began closing the doors of our meetings at the time they were scheduled to start. If you were late, you weren't allowed to enter until there was a break. That's accountability. And when we had a charter flight, it left when it was scheduled to leave. We didn't wait for stragglers, and several times we took off while a latecomer ran out waving his arms as we took flight.

We also sought solutions that were wins for both companies or that at a minimum would be a win for one with little or no cost to the other.

There's an old saying that expresses our challenge: if you want results never before obtained, then you need to use methods that have never before been employed. The goal was to create sustainable competitive advantages for both companies, while furthering our respective leadership positions in our industries. In that respect, we wanted to be seen as the gold standard when it came to supplier-retailer partnerships.

Our joint vision was to demonstrate that what we could accomplish together as a team would be unprecedented in scope and depth. This would make us a model for future customer-supplier relationships but also challenge universities to use our success in their industry research and eventually in their curriculum offerings.

And, in fact, we were able to bring our new reality forward in ways that helped several universities create multifunctional business courses. We helped them understand the importance of the different elements of the relationship—things like our approach to supply chains or shopper marketing—and that influenced courses in which the P&G team sometimes taught or contributed as guest lecturers.

We also shared much of what we learned in our work with Walmart in ways that benefited other suppliers if it served the good of the retail industry and consumers. This wasn't a disadvantage to us, because we were constantly in a mode of moving forward and reinventing in ways that kept us ahead of the competition.

Servant Leaders Serving Leaders

Our unique identity as a team was always a result of our efforts to find the best ways to deliver on our team mission, which, of course, was part of P&G's mission. None of this happened by accident; it was a reflection of the intentional efforts of our leadership team.

For instance, the core leaders of the customer service team worked hard to stay unified, and we were very protective of people on the ground in Arkansas. That helped us create our desired culture and shelter it from influences that might cause friction. Like parents with their children, we often protected the team from the battles we faced internally at P&G's headquarters. And we did our best to be the ones who communicated discipline and corrective feedback when it was necessary.

We operated on a servant leadership model, which owes its origins to the life and teachings of Jesus. It gained momentum in the business community in the 1970s thanks to the writings of Robert Greenleaf, but in the 1990s it was still considered a novel approach.

Rather than using the traditional hierarchical pyramid with executives at the top, we flipped things so the leaders were serving the rest of the organization. Our role was to help remove roadblocks, provide the right tools and resources, help people develop, reward people for their work, break logjams, and always lead with the best interests of the individual and the team in mind.

One of the ways this played out was with popcorn talks.

I started work very early every day, and around 3 p.m. I typically found my mind wandering. Usually it was leading me toward a snack, so I'd make a fresh bowl of microwave popcorn, take a walk down the halls, and randomly pop in for visits with people to talk about the top problems they were working on.

What I initially found, aside from someone hiding under a desk to avoid giving me bad news, was that they assumed it was going to be a conversation on performance. They didn't realize I was there to help.

So during a team meeting I asked everyone to write the top three problems they are trying to solve on the whiteboards in their offices. That would help them stay focused on the big stuff, but it also made it much easier for me when I showed up with my popcorn. I could offer them a snack and go to the whiteboard to see where I could help. The whiteboards also helped the team serve each other when they held meetings in each other's offices.

It was a real game changer for our culture, and it created a new phrase in the team vocabulary—"What does help look like?" It was much more enjoyable for me to talk about the problems we were trying to solve.

One day, for instance, I came into Jesse Edelman's office, popcorn in hand, and asked "what help looked like" with that data analysis he was doing.

"If I just had a faster computer the results would be better and it would take much less time," he said.[4]

I asked what he meant, so he demonstrated by typing in some information and asking the computer to crunch it into something useful. Then we waited and waited and waited for the computer to digest and process the data. Point made.

In the hierarchical structure of P&G, the newest and fastest computers always went to the folks highest on the organization's leadership chart, so I had a top-of-the-line machine that I hardly used for anything but sending email.

"Jesse, I'm about ready to make your day," I said. "If you can make your computer do my email, I will give you my computer, which is way faster than yours."[5]

We completed the trade on the spot and, of course, the word quickly circulated through the team about this story. From then on, it was amazing how much response I got when I asked, *What does help look like?* They had the confidence to tell me, and I'd estimate that 80 percent of what they needed was within my scope of authority to provide.

We also were very open about objectives, information, results, and priorities.

Our Monday morning huddle meetings, which were our take on Walmart's Saturday morning meetings, lasted about an hour and were one way we kept the communication line open and modeled the culture.

I would dictate relevant points from the Walmart meeting I had just attended, and my wonderful administrative assistant Anna Weaver would come in very early on Monday morning to transcribe it. She had it in everyone's inbox an hour before our huddle meetings. She had the habit of making me look much better than I deserved.

At one of our meetings, I took an idea from Dan Cathy, CEO of Chick-fil-A, and bought some shoeshine brushes with "WGCT" (Walmart Global Customer Team) printed on them. When the meeting began, I had the leadership team come forward and I got on my knees and shined all their shoes. Then I gave each of them a brush, and they did the same thing for their teams.

Everyone on the team then got a brush so that they could do the same for others they worked with and to have as a memento to commemorate the example of how we expected our team to operate.

We also adopted Walmart's willingness to poke fun at the team leadership, so we had a lot of laughs as well as serious business building and innovation development. And when we had record months with our business results, which was often in those early years, we celebrated with lunches where the leadership team cooked and served the rest of the team.

A company can never replace a family, but because we all were new to the region and finding our way together, we definitely developed a family-like culture. We held events throughout the year that included team members' families, and new team members were welcomed to the area with homemade baked goods on the day they moved in.

If someone experienced a personal speed bump in life, we were quick to reach out with help. And we worked hard to make sure people knew each other personally, because that's what led to a caring, supportive culture when times got tough, personally or professionally.

In fact, when someone new had been on the team for two weeks, I would invite them into my office to find out how they were doing with work and how things were with their family. Then I would say, "By the way, have you met the receptionist and the person who cleans the toilets and makes sure that every day when we come in things are clean?" Most would say, "No, I haven't." Then I would say, "Why don't we meet again next Friday after you've had a chance to meet and introduce yourself to both of them." (Appendix D is a copy of my personal operating philosophy and expectations, which I gave to all new hires.)

We also had a more formal, robust onboarding program to help new team members adapt and contribute quickly. All new management-level team members, for instance, spent time working in multiple departments of a Walmart store, and some visited a Walmart distribution center. And for the first few years, our team members attended the Walton Institute training for their first-level managers.

Whenever new team members arrived, they quickly got involved in local organizations and took part in community events, all of which allowed our culture to extend beyond our business roles. We weren't parachuting in and looking for a way to get home. We were home.

Growing Careers

People want to be part of something bigger than themselves, and we all have an innate desire to contribute and see our fingerprints on the final results.

The Walmart Customer Team provided that opportunity because, unlike companies where people are pigeonholed into specific roles or functions, we intentionally developed a culture that encouraged people to take risks on new ideas but also to learn new skills and play different roles. We found that people's lives were changed when they were given the opportunity to be part of something bigger that included opportunity, skill development, encouragement, and recognition.

We believed people deserved more than a paycheck, so we committed to supporting our team not only in their professional work but in whatever ways we could with the speed bumps in their personal lives. We wanted them to grow personally and professionally, and we wanted them to get credit for their accomplishments.

For instance, many of our projects were led by someone in the middle or even on the first level of the organization. Those of us on the leadership team who were part of such projects would answer to those leaders, regardless of their organizational rank.

While we all had different roles with different pay based on our responsibilities, we highlighted the importance of each role and each individual. Like the different parts of the human body, we all had different functions but we all were important to the overall health and success of the team.

We also often put team members in roles that were new to their careers, including roles we created that didn't previously exist. This was deliberate so we could get fresh thinking and so we could develop additional skill sets, procedures, and processes in the team.

For instance, Harry Campbell had a brand management background, which meant he was from marketing. His natural career course would have been a promotion to brand manager of a specific product. But he moved to Arkansas and we gave him sales responsibilities. And instead of a promotion to brand manager, we promoted him to group marketing manager, which just meant he had sales and marketing responsibilities on our newly created customer business development (CBD) team for Walmart.

Later, Harry went back to Cincinnati as a brand manager, but he soon moved out of P&G for other opportunities.

"I had such a downer after leaving the Walmart team because of the camaraderie of the experience," Harry said.[6]

The culture was unique, he recalled, because for the first time he had the freedom to make things up on the fly and "backfill with data to make sure you were doing the right thing." He also was able to work with and learn from a wide range of experienced, senior leaders.

"P&G was very regimented at the headquarter level, particularly when it came to the idea of dealing with anybody above your boss," he said. "Whereas the Walmart Customer Team was very flat. And so the ability I had to be around senior leaders to absorb not just what they were doing, but how they led and how they got things done with their counterparts at Walmart was phenomenal. I'll forever be grateful for what I was able to learn."[7]

Henry Ho, meanwhile, went from a supply chain role to CBD.

"I was put into big soap, which is the biggest division P&G had," Henry recalled. "Can you imagine how they saw that internally? Who is this Henry Ho guy? But I was here and I got trained up as a CBD guy, not a sales guy, because we wanted people who understood the customer and the company. It made people nervous back in Cincinnati."[8]

Maybe so, but Henry knew how P&G operated, understood Walmart and Sam's Club (which was his customer), and thought systematically, which was exactly what we needed. And not only did he win the Chairman's Award (for sales) twice, but later he led one of our multifunctional Walmart teams in China.

These broadening assignments sent a very powerful signal about the upward mobility you could have by working on our team, not only in your function but across the team.

To create this aspect of our culture and attract the type of talent we needed, we had to reinvent P&G career paths. CBD didn't exist before we started this team, so it had to become something people wanted to move into, and it had to provide them a path to something better as they advanced in their careers.

We convinced the marketing department, for instance, that an assignment on the Walmart team gave their people the experience with retailers they previously got by spending time in sales. Likewise, the finance department traditionally required its people to work in a plant or take some other assignment outside the headquarters to broaden their experience and move up in their careers. They could get that experience with us.

P&G typically gave people assignments that were predetermined to last two or three years, so we also developed a system of promoting people into new levels or new roles so we could keep them on our team longer and build continuity. Over the years, new titles were created and the opportunity to work on a multifunctional team provided a career path to senior management.

At one point, in fact, I was told I was in line for a promotion to vice president. A CBD team leader, however, couldn't be a vice president. I was told I needed to move to Caracas to be the sales vice president of Latin

America and South America if I wanted the promotion. I declined and pointed out that I thought other companies would hire me in that role if P&G wasn't interested. Eventually, although certainly not immediately, I got that promotion, and without moving to Venezuela.

Promotions were part of a culture of rewards and recognition. We focused on creating heroes—identifying superior performances and superior efforts throughout the team. We came up with all sorts of awards to honor team members who did something significant. We even rewarded failure. Tom Verdery, an early group marketing manager, in fact, called the Failure Award one of the greatest awards he ever received at P&G.

"It was a restaurant certificate for a dinner for two to thank me for trying to convince P&G to try a new concept that the leadership team knew had potential," Tom said. "The impact of that little reward was to accelerate my testing and keep pushing for that next breakthrough idea."[9]

We also honored those who left the team for other roles within P&G or for opportunities with noncompetitors, because they deserved the acknowledgment but also because we wanted their work to inspire others and we wanted to encourage them to stay connected.

All these years later, I hear from former team members like Jesse Edelman, who told me his most prized business possessions include the Chairman's Club Award (1992), the Gold Club Trophy (1993), and a framed copy of our team operating principles. Or Harry Campbell, who was among many who took part of the University of Arkansas sports culture with him when he left.

"I got to be so much of a fan that when I left one of my parting gifts was a basketball signed by all the Razorbacks from the Final Four team of 1990," Harry said. "A plaque on it said 'the Arkansas experience.' I've still got that in my office here because I became a huge Razorback fan. I had one of those crazy hog hats, and I would call the Hogs. Coach Nolan Richardson was awesome, and the team was great. And all this, from a culture standpoint, I just loved it."[10]

We took great satisfaction in pushing the possible even in small areas. While many companies introduced casual Friday, we decided to go 100 percent business casual unless we had a meeting at Walmart Home Office. Our rationale was that we sold laundry products, and if more companies followed us it would be great for our business.

One of our Sam's Club team leaders, Joe Quinn, pushed the envelope even beyond my comfort level as an early mover to the "working remote" trend. He used the Atlanta Bread Company as a locale for meetings with his team members. I wasn't a big supporter of the concept, so after a brief test period, we strongly urged Joe to return to the team office full time.

Evolving the Culture

The culture of the Walmart Customer Team evolved with time. Both companies grew, our team grew, and the market dynamics changed. The fundamentals of the brand that resulted from our culture, however, didn't change dramatically. We just added clarity to how we described it.

In 2001, for instance, we created a directional vision document that showed the front of a building (see appendix C). At the top was our mission: to deliver to the shopper.

The four supporting columns, essential to holding up the roof, were our key stakeholders: our company (P&G), our customer (Walmart), the individuals on our team, and the team as a whole. The columns were anchored in a bedrock layer of core values like showing respect, working strategically, innovation, mutual interdependence, and seeking to be the best.

Such ideals served us well during my leadership tenure, and I believe they still serve the team and relationship well to this day. How so? Well, in much of the rest of this book, I will share examples of how the team lived out that aspirational culture to produce unprecedented results that exceeded even our own lofty expectations.

The culture alone, however, wasn't enough; the other daunting task was to put the right structures in place to support the work, and there was no existing blueprint for what we wanted to build.

Notes

1. Lou Pritchett, speaking notes, May 30, 1989.
2. Mike Milligan, speaking notes, September 1989.
3. Milligan, speaking notes.
4. Jesse Edelman, interview with the author, 2023.
5. Edelman, interview.

6. Harry Campbell, interview with the author, 2023.

7. Campbell, interview.

8. Henry Ho, interview with the author, 2023.

9. Tom Verdery, interview with the author, 2023.

10. Campbell, interview.

CHAPTER 13

Sharing the Story

The team we assembled in the late 1980s went to work with the belief that we were transforming the way P&G would interact with all of our retail customers, starting with Walmart, and that the company would never go back to the old ways of doing business. The success of the collaboration rested on nothing short of our full commitment to that belief, and so that's the way we operated.

At the same time, we were well aware as a leadership team that nothing was guaranteed and that our survival depended on gaining long-term and widespread buy-in from leaders at all levels of both companies, which, of course, would depend largely on the quality of our results and our ability to communicate them in an engaging, open, and transparent manner.

As Don Bechtel, our mirror team leader for product supply, put it, "We were on probation from the get-go. There were a lot of naysayers waiting to see how long it would take for us to fail."[1]

The way I saw it, we weren't just selling P&G products to Walmart, we were selling a new approach to business to everyone—our team, Walmart, and, perhaps most importantly, the decision makers within P&G. So while we had to produce positive results, we also had to share our story in ways that created commitment and built momentum.

Everyone involved needed to see that all this collaborative disruption was worth the discomfort that comes with change. They needed to understand and believe in the vision the same way we did, or else they'd never develop a passion for it and they would give up rather than push through when things weren't going as planned.

Our few early supporters needed to know that they had backed a winning horse, and others—those who had legitimate concerns, those who were indifferent, and as many of the skeptics as possible—needed to see how and why they would benefit and how they were important to a burgeoning success story.

Among our first and biggest efforts to share the story took the form of the infamous Year One Report—a comprehensive review of our team's first fiscal year (1988–89). Our hope was that this report would convince the P&G world (or at least our part of it) that the one-company model should evolve from a "test" to a permanent way of going to market.

The report covered every aspect of the business we were working on with Walmart and Sam's Club, and in considerable detail. We explained where things were when we started, where they were now, how we got there, the issues we still needed to resolve, and where we saw the relationship in the years to come.

We provided the big-picture numbers like the increases we'd made in a year in terms of sales volume and gross sales, and we dove deeply into the minutiae of as much data as we could collect. There were around fifteen tabbed sections, and each was filled with numbers about the performance of every function represented on our team and the business impact for every product division.

When I asked Don Bechtel about his memories of the Year One Report, his brutally honest reaction was that "it was a lot of work" and many on our team weren't sure it was worth the effort.

"Initially, there was a fair amount of resistance on the team because I don't think we all had the vision about how effective it could be to communicate not just to P&G, but to the Walmart organization," he said.[2]

Mike Graen referred to it as "a painful document" but added, "It basically did celebrate a lot of things that we had gotten done in a relatively short period of time."[3]

And that was the point—to share and celebrate those early successes and the people who made them possible while also painting a vision of what was possible in the future.

We sent the books in advance to all the functional heads and to the vice presidents of each of the product divisions and their key leaders. We then met as a team with the leadership groups of each of the product divisions. We reviewed the results, answered questions, and frequently made recommendations about better ways to do things in the future.

Some of these meetings became heated because the leaders in a few business units didn't want to make the changes that we were recommending.

For instance, we recommended that we change the department of the people on the team from sales to customer business development (CBD). Language is important, and the change provided a better description of the multifunctional team concept and delineated it from the traditional sales organization. It was also a much more positive concept with Walmart, because it was more about working together than about Walmart doing something just for our benefit.

After brutal discussions and pushback from the product divisions on making this a permanent structure, on the name change, and on the request for additional resources, the tide, so to speak, began to turn when we met with the packaged soap and detergent unit, commonly known as PS&D.

John Smale, our CEO, slipped into a seat at the rear of the room during the meeting and listened to the back-and-forth bantering of our contentious discussion. About twenty minutes later, John stood and the room fell silent.

This is no longer a test, he told the gathering. The results are strong enough that it makes sense to expand with Walmart and to consider expanding to other important customers. Furthermore, he added, it would be much more beneficial for everyone if we spent the rest of our time working together on the best ways to expand it rather than debating whether it's going to be expanded because that decision had already been made.

Later (while writing this book, in fact), I learned that P&G executive vice president Gerry Dirvin had been working on our team's behalf with John Smale. Gerry was John's trusted confidant with a sales background, and his behind-the-scenes support was more important than we knew at the time. You don't always know where your help will come from.

This type of executive sponsorship and legislate-from-the-top leadership wasn't common at the time at P&G, so it was a powerful show of support. Our team could hardly contain ourselves. We had been through a very difficult week during which we were challenged at every corner, but the results and the concept prevailed.

Before we left town, I was invited to join John and a few other key leaders—Tom Laco, our vice chairman; Mike Milligan, our global vice president of sales; and John Pepper, president of the US division—to discuss how to move forward, what new resources we could expect, and how this idea would be expanded to other important customers.

We also needed to develop a better process for working with the functions and the business units so that we were not constantly fighting. I'll share more about that later, because it will take an entire chapter, but the Year One Report gave us a head start by emphasizing the need to share our results and celebrate those who made them possible.

Beyond Lip Service

Communication gets plenty of lip service in the business world, and it comes up over and over for two reasons: One, effective communication is essential to every organization's success. And two, effective communication is really hard to do well, most companies don't do it well, and, therefore, it's always an issue.

The truth of those realities multiplies faster than bunnies on a rabbit farm when you are talking about the collaboration between companies. Fortunately, we had learned a great deal about communication from our days as a design team that was researching new ways of going to market, reviewing them with the steering team, and then trying to sell our conclusions within P&G. We recognized the importance of regular, planned, and thoughtful communication within P&G and with Walmart, and we had some ideas about how to make it happen.

Walmart, in fact, was a critical audience when it came to the Year One Report (and subsequent annual reports). We shared drafts with our counterparts on their team and the final polished version circulated among their executives, just as it was circulated throughout P&G.

The annual report, however, was just one part of the puzzle. We had to create a variety of communication pieces that achieved different objectives with specific stakeholders throughout both organizations.

P&G was very much a written culture that thrived on one-page memos and one-page issue sheets, while Walmart communicated more with real-time results and through verbal communication like discussing issues and opportunities at their Saturday morning meetings. So we developed visual, verbal, and written communications, all with the objective of giving people an opportunity to talk, listen, understand, be involved in the plans, and see the results.

The members of our multifunctional team, for instance, wrote quarterly letters that were distributed throughout their functions at the P&G headquarters in Cincinnati. These letters included a broad list of lessons they had learned, things they had done, implications of decisions they had made, new ideas they were considering, and requests for testing or additional resources.

"We always said the hardest part of a sales team is selling back internally," said Henry Ho, who helped build our customer service team for Walmart. "So each of the functional leaders of the team had to go sell their respective line bosses to sell the changes we were conjuring up to improve the business."[4]

The letters also became a valuable development tool because they helped account executives and functional leaders improve as business writers.

To improve the link to results between the categories and Walmart, we created an eighteen-month planning cycle that enabled us to accommodate the differences in the two company's fiscal years (P&G's ended in June, while Walmart's ended in January).

We followed up the letters with quarterly face-to-face meetings with our team and the category general managers and their teams. These meetings included me and the functional leaders from our team, plus the category team members who were dedicated to the business we were discussing.

In some cases, representatives from Walmart were part of these meetings. In fact, sometimes we would hold regional meetings in cities like Dallas or Atlanta, and Walmart would contribute to the agenda, which typically included visits to their stores and their competitors' stores.

The quarterly meetings allowed for reviews of the previous quarter's results and what we had learned during that time. We made tweaks to our plans for upcoming quarters and introduced elements of the new quarter that was fifteen months in the future. The meetings unlocked enormous creativity and used the combined talents and resources at P&G with those at Walmart to really bring the one-company operating model to life with incredible results.

These meetings allowed Walmart direct access to our category leaders and gave those leaders access to Walmart. Account executives and buyers still played key roles in our business results, but we reduced the odds that they might misunderstand or misquote information in areas where they weren't the experts.

When we agreed to a new idea or to test something, we were better aligned on what we were going to do and the criteria each company would use to measure success. We also developed robust scorecards that reflected the criteria important to both companies, and we provided written summaries of what we had agreed to, the next steps, and who was responsible for each action and on what timing.

Our account executives also produced quarterly results by buyer, which we could circulate to the buyers' supervisors within Walmart to show how they had participated in programs and the implications for Walmart's results. The buyers often used these in their performance reviews to demonstrate how they took initiative and delivered results.

As the team leader, I also provided a monthly letter that went into great detail about business results and highlighted every individual business unit or function. My letter had a very broad distribution, including all the senior executives of the company.

These communication efforts held us accountable as a team, but also provided opportunities to raise and address issues. And they motivated the category and product divisions that would notice strong results from other business units. Their leaders wanted to share in the spoils, so it opened the door for us to sit down and say, "OK, here's what you have to provide if you want those kinds of results." Our motto was that while we were good, we could not make gold out of straw, and we couldn't allow them to eat at Ruth's Chris and pay McDonald's prices!

Top to Top

Communication between top executives remained vital to the success of the one-company model, and while written reports were important, nothing could take the place of face-to-face interactions between the senior management of the two companies.

This not only helped the top leaders align on what was going on and what we needed to ensure our future success, but it was a way of moving information and motivation through both organizations.

We also invited nonsenior leaders on our teams to make presentations, answer questions, and get feedback on their projects, which was both very motivating and a great development process for them to see what it was like to be in the limelight and the hot seat simultaneously.

We had top-to-top meetings that involved the CEOs and presidents of the various divisions of Walmart and P&G, but we also brought together functional leaders. Walmart's top leaders in finance like the CFO, treasurer, tax experts, and senior analysts, for instance, would meet with their counterparts from P&G, sometimes in Arkansas and other times in Ohio.

The CFOs, in fact, would touch base prior to calls with external market analysts. They shared what they were seeing in the marketplace, which helped shape their conversations and ensure they weren't providing information that would cause the other company a problem without them knowing about it in advance.

Additionally, I had a bimonthly meeting with Walmart's CEOs from the time the team started through my retirement. Those typically were lunch meetings where we ate sandwiches in their office and reviewed results of the partnership, shared ideas and plans we were working on, and discussed goals for the coming months. This also was when I typically learned about new initiatives Walmart had in the works, which allowed us to consider ways P&G might help them make those ideas a reality.

Occasionally, a meeting won't go as planned, such as when our team created an early artificial intelligence application using data from Retail Link. We referred to it as the "black box" and introduced the idea at a top-to-top meeting with Walmart CEO David Glass and P&G CEO Ed Artzt. In our enthusiasm, however, we forgot to get advanced alignment from Bobby Martin, Walmart's senior vice president of IT. We ended up confusing both CEOs and irritating Bobby. We had to eat considerable quantities of humble pie to restore his trust—our version of a "clean up in aisle 4."

All of these communication efforts, however, didn't eradicate all of the resistance we faced. We still had to face the dragons that are common to almost any significant effort to bring about transformative change.

Notes

1. Don Bechtel, interview with the author, 2023.
2. Bechtel, interview.
3. Mike Graen, interview with the author, 2023.
4. Henry Ho, interview with the author, 2023.

PART III

Battling the Barriers

Before the ink is dry on any vision, you'll encounter challenges and barriers. You'll have to get good at eating problems for breakfast. The secret is to confront challenges head-on with tenacity and a mindset that all obstacles can be overcome in a way that benefits everyone involved.

CHAPTER 14

Walk toward the Barking Dog

Long before anyone coined the term "last-mile delivery," the news of the day was printed on large sheets of paper and then rolled into something that looked like a small campfire log so it could be delivered directly to the homes of people who were eager to read it.

Some newspapers were delivered in the mornings and others in the afternoon, but either way, the last-mile delivery made for a great part-time job for any youngster with a bicycle and a modicum of ambition.

I had a paper route when I was growing up in both Dubois, Pennsylvania, and Maumee, Ohio, but it wasn't enough to throw the *Pittsburgh Press* or the *Toledo Blade* in the driveways or on the sidewalks of my customers' homes—I walked up and placed it between the screen door and the front door. Even then I was all about customer service!

This typically was an uneventful experience, but sometimes— too often, in fact—I was greeted by an unfriendly dog that shared its displeasure by ferociously barking its dang head off. I had two choices: I could run, or I could walk toward the barking dog.

When a dog is barking at you, running seldom keeps you from getting bitten. A really mean dog will chase you, and the dog can run faster than you can. In the end, it gets you. But if you walk toward the barking dog, most of the time it will back off and back down.

During my time as our team leader, this became a go-to metaphor whenever we faced tough problems—which was almost daily. Problems don't go away by ignoring them, running from them, or hoping no one will notice them. Hope is not a strategy. You needed to face them and deal with them. And to do that, we had to walk toward the barking dog.

The bigger the problem, the more likely some folks are to ignore it. They keep themselves busy with anything they can to distract them from the elephant in the room—or what I preferred to call the moose on the table.

We walked toward the barking dog. We addressed the elephant in the room. And we dealt with the moose on the table.

It was sometimes like we were running around in a zoo!

Principles over Policies

Leaving all metaphors aside, which I do begrudgingly, our strategy was to acknowledge the issues, determine which ones were worth solving and in what sequence, and then take them on one bite at a time with a commitment to principles over policies.

Policies emerge in companies to ensure consistency in best practices and ways of working that save time since the same situation doesn't have to be rethought each time it comes up. When you are doing something brand new, however, some policies can become barriers. The secret isn't in abandoning all the policies but in defaulting to principles where policies aren't helpful.

We had some big issues in the early years. This was a radically new way of doing business for the two companies, and we both could be set in our traditional ways and proven policies. But we discovered how "iron sharpens iron" and that we could disagree without being disagreeable or parochial. When we identified an issue and let principles drive the discussion, we inevitably found solutions that were good for Walmart and P&G.

When such issues arose in the relationship, my go-to preface to the discussion was the following:

- Let's focus on the issues rather than our positions or current policy.
- Let's determine what's right rather than argue over who's right.
- Once we have all the cards on the table face up, we can work out a solution that's a win for both companies and is principle based.

I found this approach tempered some of the emotions going into a discussion where we were starting from very different points of view. It also provided a solid rationale to get the issue resolved internally if that was required to move forward.

Most of the time, the issues weren't resolved by using the P&G way or the Walmart way but by inventing a third way that made more sense given all the factors that had to be satisfied and that would meet and exceed the expectations of both companies.

Let's look at a few examples.

Pringles, Part II

Perhaps the biggest moose on our table when we began the relationship with Walmart involved our different strategies for pricing products.

Walmart revolutionized the retail industry with its strategy of everyday low prices, but not without significant resistance from consumer product companies like P&G. Our model, a "high-low" strategy, involved offering temporary price reductions and promotions. This enticed retailers to give our promoted products favorable displays in their stores, but it meant the prices often were fluctuating—for Walmart and for consumers.

If we gave Walmart an average price for the year so they could sell a product at an everyday low price, we feared they would have no incentive to favorably merchandise our products.

Walmart countered that our brands would get prominent displays because they were the market leaders and, therefore, their pricing strategy would be to our advantage. Our product division vice presidents were skeptical of Walmart's promise of continued merchandising of our brands without a contract binding them to performance requirements before we would pay the merchandising money.

Walmart also pointed out that if customers could buy our products whenever they were in the store, rather than waiting on a promotion, they would know they were getting a good price and then it would increase our business. They also hypothesized that everyday low prices would improve inventory management for both companies and lead to more efficient manufacturing on the P&G end.

Furthermore, they pointed out that retailers often bought far more product than they needed from P&G when P&G was offering a promotion. In a common industry practice known as "forward buying," they stocked their stores, but kept the rest in a warehouse until the promotion ended. Then they used it to restock their stores and sold it at a higher price and higher margin. This meant we were overpaying for the merchandising, and it made it challenging for us to predict demand. Our factories ended up going through feast-or-famine cycles that were terribly inefficient.

Walmart challenged us to look at how shoppers actually bought products and then evaluate the total effect that a more balanced pricing strategy would have on our system. As a result, we were willing to consider putting our toe in the water.

This journey began, as you might recall, with the early experiment with Pringles as Sam Walton's volume producing item. Based on that success, we added more brands with a retailer choosing either a high-low promotion program or an everyday low price promotion program.

As we rolled out more and more categories with Walmart, they continued to support our brands in store with displays, and we saw that our business responded well to the everyday low price program plus the merchandising.

Payment Terms

P&G offered a discount to customers like Walmart if they paid their invoices within a certain time period, but each P&G product division had different terms for those discounts.

One might give the discount if Walmart paid within ten days, for instance, while another might pay it if Walmart paid within thirty days. It was easy for Walmart to get confused and pay the wrong amount since all the invoices said Procter & Gamble. This misalignment resulted in calls, time, and paperwork to get it corrected.

It also created a good bit of ill will between the people involved.

When we learned how big this issue was, P&G created an internal group to evaluate consolidating the terms offered by all of our product divisions. It was a massive assignment that involved things like an analysis of the cash flow implications and the competitive advantages and disadvantages any changes might create.

Eventually, this team harmonized all P&G payment terms to seventeen days. Initially, there were some negative cash flow issues, but over time it proved to be a cost-neutral change for P&G and a big win for us with Walmart, with other retailers, and internally at P&G because of the major reduction in rework to correct the misalignment.

Damaged Goods

Walmart's customer-friendly approach to returns and P&G's emphasis on customer satisfaction resulted in policies for each company that were built on the same principle: valuing the customer. In practice, however, those policies created issues that became a moose on the table.

In those days, Walmart took damaged P&G products from their stores, sent them back to a warehouse, and charged P&G for the reimbursement of the damaged products by putting a deduction on the invoice of a future order.

After a fair amount of research on those deductions, we noticed that we often were charged for empty diaper packages that were marked as "box knife damage." When we investigated further, we realized a number of Walmart stores were providing free diapers in their women's restrooms that came from what they considered to be damaged goods because of "box knife" cuts. Then they sent the empty packages back to the warehouse for us to provide credit.

At the same time, P&G was investing millions of dollars to improve our packaging with the goal of reducing damage to our products, much of which occurred in shipping.

We scheduled a meeting with Walmart to discuss our position versus theirs. We couldn't pay for store damage if the products were actually being used in the store, such as with the diapers or with cleaning products used to clean stores. It was a very messy, intense discussion at the time, but we came to a common point of view based on the principle of fairness.

It was fair for us to compensate them for P&G products that were damaged when they arrived at the store, and fair for them to take responsibility for damages that happened within the store or for other uses of products in their stores.

In-Store Thefts

When Walmart began experiencing an increase of thefts involving some high-priced health and beauty items like razor blades and certain cosmetic brands, they requested a meeting with leaders from P&G and Gillette to discuss the issue.[1]

Tom Coughlin, who was the president of Walmart stores, and Doug Degn, the executive vice president of merchandising at Walmart, wanted us to put anti-theft devices on these products that would alert store security if someone tried to leave without paying for an item.

Back then, attaching those devices was an expensive, manual process. While it made sense for items like televisions or computers, we weren't keen on the idea of attaching them to every pack of razors or every jar of face cream. And in addition to that expense, it would disrupt our entire manufacturing process.

The conversation was tense and heated, and Walmart suggested that they would have to lock the products in a secure area or discontinue carrying some of them if we didn't add the security devices.

At the time, P&G and Gillette were part of a consortium of suppliers working with MIT on what was then a new-to-retail technology known as RFID (radio-frequency identification) tags. These tags held digitally encoded data that could be read using electromagnetic waves, and, among other things, they held the promise of a more inexpensive way to monitor a high-volume product.

Tom and Doug agreed to fly with me to Boston to learn more about the project. And as an olive branch of goodwill, they had me join them on a Walmart company plane to get there.

We spent a day and a half at MIT and they saw the potential of the technology, so we suggested they join the consortium. They would be the only retailer involved, which would give them an opportunity to shape the execution that cascaded from the research. But to them it was a "future solution to a present problem."

This left us with two issues: we needed an immediate cost-effective way to reduce thefts on the P&G and Gillette products, and we wanted Walmart's involvement in the RFID project.

Walmart was unwilling to pay the stiff annual fee to join the consortium, so we agreed to fund the first year from a "test and learn" budget. If they found it beneficial, they would pay the fee after that.

For the second issue, we agreed to increase the size of our packaging for certain products to make it more difficult for would-be thieves to slip the items in their pockets. It wasn't a perfect solution, but it was a step forward in a responsible way.

As it turned out, RFID technology wasn't the solution to in-store theft we thought it might be, but it proved to be a huge innovation in supply chain management. The tags are used to track product movements in shipping and trucking, as well as in factories and warehouses. They also are used for things like toll collections.

Walmart now uses RFID in their stores and distribution centers to track suppliers' items. Suppliers put the RFID tags on the items, and they can track items all the way through the supply chain. Over 60 percent of the merchandise in a Walmart store in 2024 has been RFID tagged. So the investments in RFID by P&G, Walmart, and other companies still paid significant benefits.

Electronic article surveillance technology, meanwhile, emerged around 1999 as a more common way to combat theft in retail stores. Readers are set up at exits and alert security if someone leaves with an item that hasn't been scanned at a register.

The point is that putting principles over policies doesn't always lead to quick, clean solutions to every problem, but it does move the discussions forward in positive ways, including ways that sometimes lead to unintended progress. And workable solutions to the original issue almost always develop along the way.

Scanning the Code

Bar codes are a ubiquitous part of products these days, but the technology has only been around since the 1970s. In 1978, in fact, fewer than 1 percent of all grocery stores in the United States had scanners, and in 1993 it was still only 60 percent.[2]

Nowadays, most customers know how to scan the code at the self-checkout, even if they might not know it's called a Universal Product Code (UPC), who invented it (IBM's George Laurer), or how it works.

Walmart has always been an early adopter of cutting-edge retail technologies, and that was the case with UPCs and scanners. I won't venture out of my lane with a bunch of technical details, but it basically works like this: the manufacturer prints the code on the product, and the scanner at a register reads the code for several pieces of information, including the price.

UPC technology is amazingly accurate, but in the early days there were a few instances of big errors that became known as the "golden chicken" and "platinum pork" problem. Those were easy enough to catch because no one was going to pay $500 for a chicken.

While most errors were small, even small errors spread over large quantities could make a big impact. So Walmart's policy was to fine consumer product companies like P&G for a bad UPC. We pushed back and eventually reached a resolution based on principles over policy.

We agreed that if the UPC error is identified when the product is still in one of Walmart's warehouses, then we should only be responsible for taking the product back and covering any cost that has incurred rather than also paying a fine. The principle: our cost should be based on the damage that Walmart incurred.

On the flip side, if a bad UPC goes into stores and, for the sake of argument, charges customers $1 for an item that should be priced at $2, Walmart could lose a lot of money. In that case, the consumer packaged goods company should be responsible for the loss from selling it at the wrong price, as well as the cost of bringing it back to the warehouse and then picking it up.

There should be no cost at all for Walmart if a consumer packaged goods company makes that kind of error. That made more sense than an arbitrary flat penalty fee for a bad UPC.

Rolling Business Plans

When we began the one-company model, Walmart's fiscal year ended in January, while P&G's ended in June. So by March of most years, Walmart already was agreeing to merchandising plans for August through the end of the year, while P&G had not yet released any promotions programs for that period because we were still in the previous fiscal year.

As a result, Walmart often took our competitors' products simply because we couldn't give them enough details for them to decide whether to take ours. So we needed a way to make promotions and products available across different fiscal years, and we did that by agreeing that both companies would operate on an eighteen-month rolling business plan.

That meant P&G would release the first six months of the new fiscal year promotion program to Walmart and to our team in March, three months before the end of the P&G fiscal year. Our team then could work with Walmart's team to make more accurate plans. We weren't able to ship products early or do anything else that would have been unfair to other retailers, but by just sharing information, we could schedule the right kind of merchandise.

This process represented a huge risk for both P&G and Walmart since both were sharing confidential information about future plans. If the details got out to either of our competitors, that would have caused major problems and potential business losses. We had signed a confidentiality agreement, but there were plenty of doubters in both companies who thought one side or the other would break it.

In my fifteen years as team leader, however, I never experienced a situation where there was any evidence of future plans being compromised. Occasionally, some of our other retail customers would run a promotion on the same P&G brand at the same time as Walmart, but that was by happenstance and based on offers that were available to everyone at the same time.

Over time, our joint teams created more of a custom plan for Walmart and other retailers using a very principle-based approach of an equal funding mechanism for all customers but latitude in how the funds were spent and on what timing.

We also began mapping when key decisions were made in both Walmart and P&G.

We were able to anticipate when Walmart would make decisions about issues involving Supercenters, Sam's Clubs, neighborhood stores, and international stores, for instance, and that allowed us to have more influence on those decisions.

Inside P&G, this mapping helped us get in front of budgeting decisions. I pitched an idea once and was told it was great but not something we could do because it wasn't in the profit forecast. This made no sense to me, so moving forward we began providing more information for the company's preliminary forecasts. Once they had it in the budget, they still could decide how they wanted to use it, but it was less likely that our ideas would get nixed simply because the money wasn't in the budget.

Protecting the Price

Instead of weekly newspaper ads with promotional specials that most retailers used, Walmart printed circulars that were inserted into hundreds of thousands of Sunday papers once a month. These circulars were produced months in advance, as were the orders for the products that would be advertised.

The long lead times helped P&G (and other suppliers) schedule our manufacturing in the most efficient way. P&G, however, had a policy that said we could increase our price at any point in time. We would honor the old price for two weeks' worth of newly purchased inventory and any immediate merchandising that was scheduled within a four-week period, but the conflict arose when we raised the price of a product that was going to be advertised a couple of months later in a Walmart circular for a lower price.

For example, if Walmart paid $10 per item and normally sold it for $11 per item, they might advertise it in their circular for $10.50 and still expect to make 50 cents on each item sold. But if P&G raised our price to $11 before the promotion began, Walmart would end up losing money on each item sold.

So we changed our policy in a way that protected orders from Walmart that were placed in good faith and well in advance, but also in a way that was beneficial to P&G.

The new policy required a firm order to be in the system to be price protected to support an agreed-to promotion. This was so important to our relationship with Walmart because they weren't buying on a high-low promotion program but rather an everyday low price program. Walmart didn't need to wait for a price promotion to schedule merchandising.

Again, it was resolved based on principle rather than policy.

We both agreed multiple times that we could argue policy versus policy and get nowhere, but we were much better off if we identified the issue that required the policy in the first place. As I suggested earlier, policies are good and useful when they are easy ways of identifying actions to take in situations that come up repeatedly. That way you don't have to think through them over and over. If the policy doesn't adequately reflect the issue, however, then it is a problem that needs to be addressed.

We accomplished this hundreds of times with Walmart, sometimes on big issues but also on smaller ones, and it improved the operations of both companies. When I asked Walmart executive Doug Degn about why the relationship with P&G was successful, he said "healthy friction," and sufficient trust allowed us to really understand the issues and explore win-win solutions. But we also had to walk toward the barking dogs within our own ranks, and sometimes those dogs were dragons.

Notes

1. This was before P&G purchased Gillette in 2005.
2. T. Seideman, "Bar Codes Sweep the World," *American Heritage's Invention & Technology,* Spring 1993, https://www.academia.edu/2484615/Bar_codes_sweep_the_world.

CHAPTER 15

Here Be Dragons

If ancient cartographers had magically given our team a map at the start
of our journey, there's no doubt it would have featured illustrations of
dragons and sea monsters.

The first mapmakers used mythical beasts as symbolic warnings of
the unknown, which to them came with inherent dangers. And we were
traveling through uncharted territory, so *hic sunt dracones* (here are dragons) often applied.

Some dangers were real. There were rough seas, rocky shores, and
unpredictable weather. The bigger problems for our team, however, came
from those who feared what might be out there, real or imagined, and
therefore preferred we stayed tethered in the harbor.

For all the incredible support we got from the admirals at the top of
both organizations and from our hardworking crew, there's no deny-
ing that we also faced significant resistance from those who imagined
dragons—and a few folks who embodied them.

By "resistance," I don't mean typical business challenges like changes
in the market conditions, policies and procedures that didn't align
between the two companies, or the problem-solving issues that come
with any innovative process.

In my experience, some of the biggest obstacles to success in a transformative partnership don't even involve the other company or the actual
process of creating something new. Instead, they come from the internal
politics and dynamics of your organization.

Simply put, fear of the unknown is an expected response in corporate environments. The desire for certainty and predictability creates an
epic tension between chaos and order that naturally results in opposition
against anyone attempting innovation.

The resistance we experienced mainly involved opposition from within P&G—from those who stayed behind and screamed, "Don't go, for there be dragons!"

Reasons for Resistance

To be fair, the resistance wasn't always from mean-spirited people with evil intentions. It also came from people with legitimate concerns, people who just didn't get the vision, those who understandably felt threatened by the changes our team was creating, and the organizational bureaucracy that had formed over the decades.

I've hit on some of the specific reasons for the resistance we experienced in previous chapters, but a few in particular are worth noting here because they are common to any multicompany partnership initiative.

One, the resistors feared that the P&G team would be co-opted by Walmart. We would forget who we worked for and focus exclusively on doing Walmart's bidding at the expense of what was best for P&G.

Two, they thought a cross-functional, customer-focused team was a dumb idea and would never work.

Three, they didn't understand the benefits, so why change?

Four, they believed the new approach would add complexity and cost to our organization.

Five, they feared a loss of control over team members who no longer reported directly to them.

Six, they thought the idea in general might work but second-guessed every decision we made. They would do it; they would just do it differently. This view always reminded me that if you want to drain a swamp, you don't rely on advice from the frogs.

And speaking of swamps . . .

The Unholy Trinity

Regardless of their motives and intentions, the resistance they created was real, and it's common to any organization of any size that's experiencing disruptive changes. Over time, I developed my own little terms to describe these phenomena.

These were descriptions, by the way, that I was using decades ago, so please don't draw any connections to how they might be used in the more current political environments. Or any political environment, for that matter. They are terms that describe the issues that show up in just about every company that exists.

The "deep state" was the folks in senior positions who controlled some of the purse strings but who didn't want to give up any of their power, authority, or ways of life. They saw change as a personal threat and were more likely to ask, "What's in it for me?" rather than, "What's best for the company and our customers?"

Our response: electricity didn't come from continuous improvement of the candle, and the automobile wasn't an evolution from the horse. Incrementalism is the worst enemy of innovation.

Members of the deep state were similar to and sometimes also members of the "flat-earth society," which was my description for the people who preferred the status quo they understood to any solutions that made them uncomfortable. They rejected almost any new idea or method if for no other reason than that it didn't fit within their established views. Dealing with them, I often said, was like talking to a mechanic who says he couldn't repair your brakes, so he made your horn louder.

Our response: you can't discover new oceans without losing sight of the shore, and no one ever erected a statue in memory of a person who left well enough alone.

The "swamp," meanwhile, was the bureaucracy that's common in almost every large organization. Policies and procedures are put in place for a reason, and those reasons typically make great sense at the time. Many policies, however, aren't dropped when they become obsolete or edited when conditions change. Instead, new policies are added on top of old ones until simple, common-sense decisions get bogged down in the muck.

Our response: the great danger isn't that our goal is too high and we miss it, but rather that our aim is too low and we reach it.

If you've ever led or been on a team with a mandate to drive meaningful change, you've probably experienced the unholy trinity of the swamp, the deep state, and the flat-earth society. And if you are involved in a transformative partnership, you need to be aware that these aren't mythical dragons or sea monsters. Dealing with them can be frustrating and discouraging, but not dealing with them is deadly to living out your vision.

What's Good for the Goose

The swamp, deep state, and flat-earth society take different forms for every innovation initiative, but a few examples of what it looked like for us can help you spot them when you see them on your map.

One of the first examples actually took place before P&G ever gave birth to the Walmart Customer Team.

Don Bechtel, our logistics expert, was a member of the original design team that researched new ways of going to market and eventually developed the idea of creating cross-functional teams that would work directly with our customers. And he reminded me of a trip we took to Dow Chemical in Detroit to get their input about how something like this might work.

Dow was one of P&G's major suppliers, not a customer, and they thought we had hit on a wonderful idea. In fact, they immediately expressed an interest in partnering with us in much the same way we ended up partnering with Walmart. We would share information with them, they would share information with us, and both companies would benefit.

That type of partnership never got off the ground, however, because too many leaders within P&G resisted the idea of sharing information with a supplier.

As far as I remember, the idea of experimenting with Dow never reached the top levels of the companies' leadership, which just shows how important it was for leaders like Sam Walton, David Glass, Don Soderquist, Lou Pritchett, John Pepper, Tom Laco, and John Smale to get involved and support the partnership between Walmart and P&G.

Once P&G's top leaders signed off on testing the multifunctional customer team concept, those who opposed it and were in power adopted a passive-aggressive approach of fighting against our efforts.

Some of the resistance was personally directed toward me and a few of our team's other top leaders. I remember one senior executive, for instance, who regularly referred to me derisively as "Tommy Walmart" and an executive vice president who would hold his fingers up to form a cross every time he saw me, as if to suggest he was dealing with a vampire. (He later became president of another company and tried to hire me as a consultant; I declined the offer.)

As senior leaders, we resolved not to let those types of petty tactics get under our skin or filter down to our team, but we had to deal directly with the challenges that would limit our ability to succeed.

For example, we approached the vice president of P&G's beauty care product division about putting some of his products in Sam's Club, and his response can be summed up in two words: absolutely not. Sam's Club, by the way, had requested the products, so it's not like we had to go sell the idea to the retail customer. But the vice president said a wholesale club was not the kind of place he wanted selling his products.

"After all," he said, "I'm in the beauty care business."

My response, which admittedly probably wasn't the most tactful, was something like, "Oh, I think I understand. You're saying only ugly people shop at club stores, and beautiful people don't want to save money."

Fortunately, our team had a partially dedicated P&G packaging expert who helped design special packaging that the vice president considered "classy" enough for us to put into club stores. These products ended up making a huge difference not only in our business with Sam's Club but also with Costco.

Another example of resistance came when we requested resources from the category product division vice presidents that were over and above what traditionally had been allocated in the sales department.

These resources were things like people to add to the team, authorization to create new roles, and financial investments for our initiatives. In any big company, people don't want to give up those types of resources unless they really understand the value to them, and these leaders struggled to see the value because they often were too far removed from the day-to-day business.

The category general managers who worked under the product division vice presidents, however, had people working for them and other resources that they could invest into building their business. And they were close enough to the business to see why our approach made sense.

They saw the kind of information we could get them from Walmart and how fast we could get it. They saw our ability to test new concepts and ideas. And they saw the business results we were generating compared to the rest of the market. Consequently, they were very happy to invest additional resources in the P&G Walmart team.

One way we earned their support was by creating low-risk, high-reward scenarios for them when we asked them to dedicate members of their teams to our team.

"They will be part of our team," we would tell them, "but they will be owned by you. So if at any point you don't think you're getting the value you should get, you can just pull back the authorization. It's a no-lose proposition for you."

Several leaders of the product divisions and functions still saw our team as an opportunity to get rid of their problem employees. Not only would they hold tightly to their best people, but they would give us their worst.

We quickly identified those poor performers and had conversations with them on how to find employment at another company. In the meantime, we continually recruited mavericks with high potential, and over time the success of the team became our strongest means of attracting the best and the brightest.

Success also armed us with data that we used to convince other resistors. We did an analysis, for instance, of what our approach to sales cost compared with the old way of doing things. Each product division back then had their own retail sales force and management structure, and they all called on most every large retailer in the United States. We showed them how much their retail coverage approach cost per case sold and compared that with our multifunctional approach with Walmart.

Our customer teams were much more efficient, the cost per case much lower, and the results far better. Eventually, they saw the logic in downsizing their retail organizations and transferring some of those resources to customer teams where they would get a much better return.

Winning in the Middle

At Walmart, there wasn't so much active resistance as doubt (*would things really change?*) and occasional resentment because test runs, new policies, and revamped procedures typically created more work for them (which was made worse when they doubted whether it would lead to long-term change).

Our approaches to the resistance within P&G, however, also helped us win over the doubters at Walmart.

In chapter 14, I talked about our efforts to communicate effectively with everyone involved, and there was no bigger factor than that when it came to overcoming the resistance of the deep state, the swamp, and the flat-earth society, or to winning over the doubters at Walmart.

We tried to capture every issue the resistors raised and then, in time, we addressed those issues with facts and results. We converted people to our point of view one person at a time and primarily from the middle of the organization. They appreciated the problems we identified and saw the opportunities for improvement, so they were willing to "slip a little bread to the prisoners." Then we tried to make them heroes by giving them credit when we shared the results that came from their support.

In general, those who were closest to the work or most responsible for the results were easier to convert because they saw and experienced the benefits more directly and personally than those who controlled the system and didn't want to take the risk of getting bad results from changing the system.

Of course, we had to get the results before we could share those stories, and one of the biggest factors when it came to overcoming resistance and achieving positive results was to give other people a clear incentive for helping our team.

Because, as I'll share in the next chapter, the problem with incentives is that they work. So you'd better get the incentives right.

CHAPTER 16

The Problem with Incentives

P aul Carter, the CFO of Walmart from 1988 to 1995, walked out of his office one morning with a cup of coffee in his hand, and I knew my moment had arrived.

In those days, I had easy access to Walmart's executive row, and I was hanging out in the area waiting for just such an opportunity. Under my arm was a large foam-board check like the ones on display at golf and tennis tournaments, so Paul naturally gave me a curious look as I walked toward him.

"I have a million-dollar check for Walmart," I said. "But I can't find anybody to take it."

"Come into my office," Paul said. "You found someone."

The oversize check prop got his attention, but now it was time to get to the real business at hand.

"OK," Paul said when we sat down. "What's the deal?"

The million-dollar check, I told him, represented an opportunity P&G and Walmart were missing by not taking better advantage of a new display program P&G created.

The innovation by P&G's packaging and manufacturing function was the development of prebuilt displays that were shrink-wrapped and placed on a pallet. P&G delivered the displays to a customer's warehouse, where it immediately was cross-docked and put on a truck to an individual store. From the truck, the pallet went straight to the end of an aisle on the sales floor, where the shrink-wrap was removed, a price sign was added, and the products were available to purchase.

The concept is common now, but no one else was doing it back then. It was a marketing and promotional game-changer because it offered tremendous savings in labor for our customers and increased the incentive to merchandise our brands. In fact, we calculated that Walmart saved 37 cents per case in handling costs by using the prebuilt displays.

What's not to like, right?

Well, the problem, as I explained to Paul, involved incentives.

Walmart buyers were required to treat these displays as brand-new items, which created a good deal of time-consuming paperwork for which they earned no reward. The savings were in the warehouses and the stores, so while the displays were a great deal for Walmart as a company, they weren't a good deal for Walmart's individual buyers.

"I can see the problem," Paul told me after I laid out the issue, "and I can fix it."

"How would you fix it?" I asked.

"If you tell me how much we would save for each one of these prebuilt display offers, we will give half of the savings to the buyers in their accounts," Paul said. "That will be a good deal for them. The other half of the savings can go to the warehouse and the store."

When the incentive system changed, Walmart's buyers began asking our team for more prebuilt displays.

For P&G, this was a great deal because it increased our in-store displays at the end of an aisle, which substantially increased our sales and our market share. We were spending additional money on the labor savings for them, but we didn't have to spend as much on price reductions and, therefore, it was a good deal in terms of both cost investment and return on investment.

This is a great example of how recognition and reward systems work. You get what you recognize and reward. That's the problem and the beauty of incentives—they work. When we started the one-company model, both companies focused on internal objectives and priorities with little or no thought to how what we wanted might impact the other. Our recognition and reward systems fostered a win-lose transactional system.

Money follows incentives, as does behavior. What is rewarded is repeated. So a key to strong partnerships is to overcome competing incentives so that your incentives create the results you actually want— positive results for both companies.

A Culture of Rewards

Few things were more important to our team than having a culture that recognized and rewarded people for behaviors that made the one-company model successful.

Our team celebrated as a group, as individuals, and as sub-teams. We recognized people who weren't on our team (at Walmart and P&G) for their contributions, and we championed those who deserved promotions, even if that meant they left our team for other assignments.

We were very sensitive to ensure that individuals from Walmart and P&G who had worked on an idea and achieved excellent results on the execution of that idea were given the proper credit. This was nothing more than what was justified and due but reinforced the benefit of spending the extra time and effort while working together on an initiative.

These awards and recognitions weren't limited to success stories. As I mentioned in chapter 12, we also had an award for failing us forward. Tom Verdery was our first recipient of this award and, as you might recall, he said it was one of the greatest awards of his P&G career.

Tom and Kirk Hessington, a Walmart buyer, "failed" by developing an idea for trial sizes for several P&G products, particularly in our beauty care division. Kirk had returned from a vacation, and he and Tom were talking about the small sizes of P&G bar soap, toothpaste, mouthwash, and shampoo in Kirk's hotel in Hawaii.

Why don't we get UPCs on these products and sell them at Walmart for travel? they wondered.

Then they figured, *Why not devote a section in every Walmart to these travel-size products?* These offerings would provide consumers with a way to sample our brands at an inexpensive price and use them for travel, and they would also increase our sales to hotels through our food, service, and lodging division.

"For the next six months," Tom told me, "I took this idea to every P&G brand manager, marketing director, and general manager that manufactured these brands in a travel size for commercial sales to hotels. I even went to the plants to see if we could place a UPC easily on each package. It was difficult to estimate the volume potential of this idea, but we knew it was significant enough to warrant a test before a national roll-out."[1]

The idea was squashed in Cincinnati because all the general managers considered it a distraction to their business. Walmart, meanwhile, worked with other consumer products companies and created a trial-size section in their stores.

While the idea didn't fly the first time through the P&G system, we celebrated Tom's initiative, creativity, and detailed recommendation in front of the entire team, and we provided him with a voucher to take his wife to a nice restaurant. We used the dinner voucher reward hundreds of times, typically with the stipulation that the winner had to tell their spouse or significant other the reason they got it and why it was important to the team.

The trial-size section proved successful for Walmart, and over time P&G added trial sizes on a number of our brands and sold them to hotels, just like Tom had recommended. We were building on the story of Thomas Edison and the number of times he failed while inventing the light bulb.

New Money

One of the most important incentives in the new relationship with Walmart involved the idea that we weren't dividing a pie but together we could make the pie bigger, or, as I liked to say, we could create new money.

In the early days, many of the skeptics and critics raised questions about profitability, most specifically about whether P&G would sacrifice profitability so that Walmart could improve their profitability. They assumed the only way we could improve their profitability was by lowering our prices to them so that they made an increased margin.

They were partly right, which made them totally wrong.

There actually were three ways we could improve a customer's profitability, and two of them were bad.

The first was by reducing our profitability and transferring it to the customer, in this case Walmart. Making that type of request to our management in Cincinnati always resulted in a brief conversation.

The second way we could improve their profits was by raising our prices by more than the cost justified and then giving part of that money back to the retailer in the form of a discount.

For instance, if we raised our price on a product from $10 to $11, Walmart would raise its price accordingly to maintain its margin. So with a 9 percent margin, it's now selling the product for $12.10 instead of $11. But because of our spend-back discount of only $0.30, Walmart's margin improves to 11.5 percent.

That's not very bright, however, because it would make us noncompetitive in the marketplace, which ultimately would reduce our sales and the profits Walmart could make off those sales.

The third option was to look for new money, which I defined as money trapped in the system and that wasn't benefiting either company or opportunities that were missed because it would take both companies working together to identify and capitalize on them.

New money is not obtained based on how big you are, but on how efficient and innovative you are. It is obtained by employing new business processes and new techniques, and by using technology and information. It is split between the partners in such a way as to reward new behaviors and actions within each company. And it is measured with data and on scorecards that relate to each company's key strategies.

The idea that the two companies working together could tap into new money was a powerful incentive to innovate, and it became more powerful as we began proving that it was possible.

For example, at the beginning of our new relationship, Walmart started out with a significant negative margin on P&G's combined brands, so our analysts used their product data by store as a gold mine of potential opportunity.

Bill Toler from P&G and Brent Berry from Walmart noticed that there were opportunities to add different sizes of certain products at different profitability from the size Walmart was carrying.

A classic example of this was with diapers (Pampers and Luvs), where Walmart was losing 16 percent on the one size of diapers they carried. We started by bringing in a second size that was larger (more diapers in the package, not bigger diapers) and suggested that Walmart price it at an 8 percent loss instead of the 16 percent loss, and we promoted that size in store with displays.

This wasn't an immediate solution, but it was a step in the right direction because every time someone bought the minus 8 percent size versus the minus 16 percent, we were significantly improving Walmart's profitability.

Brian Barkocy, one of the analysts who ran the numbers on the potential benefits of adding double packs of diapers, recalled being in the meeting when our team showed the data on a presentation slide. The buyer's supervisor got up, left the room, called the home office, and gave instructions for every store to display the double packs of diapers. Then he came back and the meeting resumed.

"That was a rush," Brian said. "We were like, 'Oh my gosh, what just happened?'"[2]

We also provided an alternative to our high-low promotion program, which I discussed in detail in chapter 14. Common pricing for the year or for extended periods of time, or what Walmart called net down pricing, fit much better with Walmart's strategy and was a step toward improving their profitability on our brands.

Another thing we did was to work with Walmart to move much faster and more aggressively when we introduced a new item, a new brand, or a brand relaunch. That substantially improved Walmart's profitability because they were getting new business before there was any kind of price cutting by other retailers.

We also improved their profitability by using their data to identify bad pricing at the store level. Walmart had a "comping" system where they lowered their price to meet a competitor's promotional price for a period of time, but often they didn't raise the price back when the competitor's promotion was over. This became a profit sieve. So we would look at what their actual price was in each of the stores versus their normal price.

We developed an elaborate system of analytics to identify these issues and then communicated that information directly to their operations managers, regional managers, or district managers, and they made the pricing adjustments in the stores.

Beyond the profitability at their store level, we found many other inefficiencies in the system that weren't benefiting either company. And by correcting those, we improved the overall profitability of both companies. That wasn't measured in the way that you would normally measure profitability. Things like improving inventory turns, which significantly improved Walmart's cash flow, had to be called out separately.

Ideas such as prebuilt displays considerably reduced the in-store and warehouse labor involved in handling our products. We also took over the ordering process, which eliminated an expense for Walmart. We took on some of Walmart's work, but we saved it in costs and better efficiencies with our suppliers and in manufacturing and inventory management.

Additionally, there were what I would call "soft benefits" from value we provided to Walmart by helping them with things like their international expansion, reorganizing their legal department, sharing data between our HR organizations, and learning from each other on training, onboarding, recognition, and rewards, which were benefits to both companies. It was difficult to put a specific price on the benefit to them, but clearly these things enhanced the relationship.

Notes

1. Tom Verdery, interview with the author, 2023.
2. Brian Barkocy, interview with the author, 2023.

PART IV

Everybody Bring
a Hammer

The one-company model works best when everyone comes ready to
do their part, even if their part isn't included in their job description.
When you see something that needs to be fixed, don't pass it off to someone else. Fix it. That attitude contributed to an innovative mindset that
never settled for ordinary results.

CHAPTER 17

Learn Fast, Fix Fast, Scale Fast

The one-company model quickly resulted in a tsunami of information, insights, and ideas, but we also recognized that we couldn't fully commit to an all-or-nothing ride on every big wave that came our way.

There are inherent risks with trying new things rather than improving existing processes. Initiatives often wipe out in spectacular fashion because the investment is too great given the level of assurance that those ideas will produce results. The fear of failure often causes organizations to move slowly or, worse, never try anything new, which is the biggest risk of all.

We were trying to get people on our team and throughout both companies to embrace the unknown, and the secret was to reduce risk through test-and-learn practices. By combining some of the best aspects of the two companies—Walmart's willingness to move fast and P&G's historical commitment to research and development—we learned fast, fixed fast, scaled fast, and made the most of new ideas in our ongoing relationship.

One key to making this happen was the approval of a nonpricing discretionary fund that I could use to pay for testing for ideas without additional trips to Cincinnati to ask Mommy and Daddy for the money. I then authorized members of the team to construct tests as well.

The Retail Link system, in particular, provided a game-changing means of collecting data, allowing us to test ideas in a few stores and compare the results with similar stores in other markets.

Analysts on our team like Rich Kley, Brian Barkocy, Jesse Edelman, John Green, and Dave Hollenbeck took mountains of point-of-sale data and gave us valuable information for improving existing business and evaluating new ideas. This gave us a far more accurate picture of what worked, what didn't work, and why, and that led to internal support for new initiatives.

Leaders of P&G's product categories became more willing to try a variety of tests because they knew we could drop ideas that didn't work with minimal loss or, as more frequently happened, tweak the ideas so that they produced the results we all wanted.

Every time we ran a test, we agreed to "success criteria" on the front end so that we could accurately assess what we did and the results. We defined a shared vision of what success would look like for Walmart, for P&G, and for consumers. If we did a test and it met P&G's criteria for success but didn't meet Walmart's, for instance, we could explore why and look for ways to fix it.

Every quarter we had a review meeting with our team, the category leaders in Cincinnati, and the Walmart team to go over results and refresh our plans. Sometimes a test didn't work because it was a bad idea, but sometimes it didn't work because we didn't execute it well. If that was the case, then we wanted to fix it and retest it. But we always had success criteria from both companies, and then we measured the results against those objectives.

This approach was cheap and fast, and it contributed to our team's mindset of informed persistence. We didn't give up on ideas too quickly because we had a process that provided proof for what worked, what didn't, and where changes might lead to improvements. And if a test was successful, we would scale quickly and with confidence. We (and Walmart) could go to our senior managers and say something like, "We tested this. It cost $5 and we got $15 back. So now we need $1 million, but you're gonna get $3 million back."

That's the sort of wave every leader wants to ride.

Making Hay with Makeup

One of our early test-and-learn success stories came in our efforts to improve the sales of cosmetics. P&G's cosmetics were highly profitable products for us and for Walmart, but they were consistently underperforming when compared with their potential, and we knew we needed to shake things up.

We had hundreds of different cosmetic products that were constantly updated with new colors, new variations, and new packaging. And most of these products came in small packages that had to be stocked in special displays.

Merchandising these products effectively took a good bit of work for the managers of Walmart's health and beauty aids departments, and it often took a backseat to other pressing issues. As a result, the products weren't upgraded and replaced as frequently as necessary, out-of-stocks were common, and sales (and profits) were low.

Bill Fields, then the senior vice president of merchandising for Walmart, told us he would send messages to the department managers encouraging them to be more diligent, but I thought the products needed more dedicated attention from a manager. So Bill agreed with me to create three test stores that would have department managers just for cosmetics. This would add an expense for Walmart, but I agreed to fund the experiment for six months from my discretionary budget.

As hoped, sales of cosmetics increased dramatically in the test stores, not only over what they had been in those stores but also over the average for cosmetics departments in all Walmart stores.

The increase to the business proved well worth the expense of adding a department manager for the cosmetics department. Bill used the test results to get approval for making this change at all of Walmart's stores, and he became a hero within Walmart in the process. And the increase in Walmart's sales of P&G's cosmetics resulted in a significant profit improvement in that brand portfolio within Walmart.

Investing in Testing

P&G's commitment to research and development—on products and on customers' habits and preferences—is legendary, and Walmart was quick to see the competitive advantage it could gain by tapping into that area of our expertise.

When their leaders visited P&G Beckett Ridge, for instance, they saw a huge warehouse that had been converted into a testing facility that included a mock grocery store where many of our suppliers provided the latest technology so that it could be demonstrated and perhaps implemented into a retailer.

We also built entire homes inside this warehouse. We had a typical Hispanic home, for instance, so we could see how it was laid out and how P&G products would be used in their normal routine. We could see if there were gaps in a product's performance based on how it typically would be used in that household. And we ran consumer focus groups in those mock homes that provided input on how products were used.

We had other homes for other demographic segments, and we also had a home of the future that had all the latest technological bells and whistles we could add.

For instance, I remember a garbage can that scanned items when they were thrown away and automatically put them on a grocery list. When there were enough items on the grocery list, an automated order went to the retailer for picking and delivery to a consumer's home. This was in the mid-1990s, so it was an amazing look into the future.

We hosted quarterly events for Walmart and other retailers so they could see what we were working on and help us jointly take advantage of what we were learning. We also walked the stores with the Walmart team, which was a great way to evaluate tests and spark ideas for new things we might cocreate.

Going for Groceries

When we first began implementing our one-company model, Walmart was primarily a general merchandising retailer. The first Supercenter opened in 1988, but most Walmart stores only had a small section devoted to food.

Based on the data, P&G knew Walmart's market share on brands like soap, detergent, and paper products—but their share on coffee was less than a tenth of what it was for those other products. So we proposed that they create a section for Folgers coffee and a selection of other products that would go with it like creamers, cups, and filters.

This experiment was successful enough that Walmart expanded its food offering to include other products like peanut butter and apple juice. And, of course, they eventually expanded their new formats that had a full commitment to the grocery business.

For P&G, the coffee experiment also led to more sales of our industrial products to Walmart. We got them to serve Folgers at their snack bars, and we ran promotions in the snack bars to promote the coffee available in the store.

EDLP and Soap

In the early stages of our partnership with Walmart, we aligned our categories with Walmart's merchandising department. For instance, bar soaps were sold in the health and beauty aid department of Walmart (and many other retailers), but they were part of another division inside P&G, the bar soap and household cleaning business.

To align with Walmart, Tom Verdery began selling all P&G beauty care products, including personal cleansing (Walmart's category name), which for P&G at that time was bar soap.

In the late 1980s, well-known P&G brands like Zest, Ivory, Camay, and Safeguard were competing with other successful brands like Dove, Dial, and Irish Spring. Our brands were still top sellers, but they were going through a decline due to the fierce competition. So we needed significant merchandising support, competitive pricing, and in-store impulse opportunities to keep shoppers from trying other brands. And thanks to great internal alignment with P&G management, the category's leaders were willing to consider another way to promote their brands at Walmart.

This turned into a perfect opportunity to test a new approach to how we used our promotional funds, and it led to the type of collaborative disruption that marked our team's efforts.

At the time, the most common practice among suppliers like P&G was to give promotion money for specific merchandising events a few times per year. These promotional funds were calculated into the price all retailers paid for the goods, no matter how frequently a retailer supported the brands.

Because of Walmart's strategy of everyday low prices (EDLP), however, much of the promotional money wasn't passed to the shopper. So we recommended that we calculate what a P&G brand would spend on retailer promotions as an average in a given time period and give that price to Walmart all the time. Furthermore, instead of incentivizing retailers to display a brand based upon promotional allowances, he suggested building plans to merchandise the brands based on an EDLP concept.

Most major manufacturers weren't willing to even test this concept in 1988 and 1989. But after several discussions with the president and general manager for bar soap at P&G and with the important support of Walt Gulick, the manager of sales promotion, this category's leaders agreed to a one-year test with Walmart.

This resulted in a huge win for both companies. Walmart had a category that was fully aligned with its EDLP strategy. And for P&G, this was the first category to truly create a separate price list equal to spending with any other customer but delivered on a day-to-day delivery of the product, not based on any required merchandising plan.

It was considered a huge risk because we were giving equal funding to Walmart without contracts to sign. After all, what if Walmart just purchased the brands and did nothing with them? To help deal with this risk, we had our first joint business planning annual agreement in bar soap. It was written down and verbally supported by both companies, but with no legal recourses if either party failed in their agreement.

So what happened?

In the first year we received national circular support every month on at least one of our brands and we had displays up the entire year on at least one brand. Tom and his team even developed a matrix with Walmart based on water softness so that Ivory would be merchandised more in areas with soft water and Zest in areas with hard water.

Our bar soap business grew over 40 percent in units sold that year, our overall market share grew to over 50 percent of Walmart's business, and Zest, for the first time in years, became the number one brand at Walmart.

The results did not go unnoticed by other categories at P&G or by our bar soap competitors. In fact, the next year all the major companies began testing EDLP with Walmart.

The Need for Speed

Walmart and P&G both experienced significant benefits when we rolled out a successful new item. Not only did the new items increase sales and profits, but the data indicated shoppers would associate the item with the retailer and return to the retailer for future purchases.

Retailers stood to gain by acting fast on profitable new items, but they could lose big if they bet on items that failed. Thus, all retailers carefully evaluated the new items that came their way to determine whether they would add it to their mix and, if so, their level of commitment. And for most retailers, this was a painstakingly slow process.

Walmart, however, recognized this as a potential opportunity with P&G because we had a proven track record for regularly introducing successful new items. Walmart's leaders had visited P&G's consumer and product research facilities, so they knew firsthand how much testing we did before we launched something new. They were willing to move more quickly on our new items because they knew the odds of success were high and the risk of failure low.

One thing stood in the way: P&G.

When we introduced a new item, we put it in distribution and got it on the shelves in stores before we began advertising—usually about sixteen weeks after a new product actually launched. This gave our competitors time to come up with a defensive program like a price reduction or a promotion.

Don Harris, Walmart's merchandising vice president, came to us and said they would take distribution in their warehouses for our new products the first day they were available for shipment. That way, by the end of the first week they would have the new product in every store, and by the end of the second week they also often had the products in a special display.

Walmart's need for speed helped us learn to introduce new items faster and more frequently. While other retailers were trying to decide if they should take our new products, Walmart already was making money on them.

This fast action from Walmart also put pressure on other retailers to move faster or yield all the profitable ground to Walmart. This faster action from other retailers was a help to P&G new item launches in general, but Walmart's willingness to move fast and the synergy between our teams proved to be a big contributor to Walmart's total profits on P&G brands.

Walmart also put the onus on P&G to make shoppers aware of new products and provide incentives to purchase even before our advertising typically began. We couldn't wait sixteen weeks. We had to innovate so we could move at the speed of Walmart.

Applying the test-and-learn model to this challenge became an important process in one of the biggest innovations in retailing—the birth of shopper marketing, a by-product of our collaborative disruption that gave rise to an entirely new way of thinking and practicing in the marketing industry. With shopper marketing, every day became our version of the Super Bowl, and not just with new products. The only question was whether we were prepared to win.

CHAPTER 18

Every Day Is the Big Game

We had been operating successfully in Arkansas for a couple of years when three individuals in the P&G marketing department, Dina Howell, Jim Bechtold, and Julie Walker, emerged as champions of making different sets of tools available to retail customers through multifunctional teams like ours.

This small group in Cincinnati was exploring ways to work with retailers so we could more effectively reach consumers who were shopping in stores. They were seen as rebels within the marketing department because their recommendations often called for sharing power with teams such as ours, which were now known as customer business development teams. These teams were in their infancy with other retailers.

The group's work was particularly relevant for the Walmart team because, as I mentioned in the previous chapter, P&G had committed to always being the first on the shelf with new items at Walmart. So we needed to understand how we could connect with shoppers when we had new items that were in the store before we could promote them with traditional advertising campaigns on television and in print.

Dina Howell, one of the rebels in Cincinnati, had done an analysis of the brand shares at Walmart and found P&G's biggest brand, Pampers, was significantly underdeveloped. So with input from P&G's chief marketing officer and the president of the Pampers division, she tried to build some co-marketing programs with Walmart to boost awareness and sales.

Those efforts led to limited success. Dina, however, saw what was happening with our multifunctional approach to Walmart, and she believed we needed to add a marketing competency to get the collaboration that was needed to take her work to the next level. She put together a proposal for adding an associate director to our team, and the marketing organization in Cincinnati supported the idea—as long as it was funded out of my budget.

I needed no convincing. The way I saw it, Walmart had more than 120 million eyeballs a week in their stores, which made every single day bigger than the NFL's Big Game. There had to be a big prize awaiting us if we could leverage P&G's marketing expertise inside those stores.

After making some adjustments on the team, I agreed to fund the role and Dina was on her way to Fayetteville, where she immediately began building relationships with key merchants at Walmart. Then she put together an initial concept on how to grow the diaper category and our market share for Pampers and presented it to Walmart's divisional merchandise manager, who at the time was Doug McMillon.

Doug, who would become Walmart's CEO in 2014, looked the presentation over and liked what he saw, but he pointed out one significant problem. "We lose money on Pampers," he told her, "and I need to focus on driving P&L to fix the margin in the category."

In other words, thanks, but no thanks.

Later that year, however, a story about Kmart's efforts to rebrand its baby department by working with the Children's Television Workshop created a lot of buzz inside the halls of Walmart. A buyer who was familiar with Dina's earlier proposal asked if she could help create a full-blown concept for the baby department that fit Walmart's brand. The catch: the buyer needed to see concepts in ten days so she could present them to her managers.

One of the first hurdles Dina faced was finding an agency to do the work. In those days, there wasn't much science or even much thought put into how to convert shoppers into buyers. Agencies specialized in things like promotions, creative advertising, design, and media, and one that could do all of that in the context of an in-store environment tuned to the shopper mindset wasn't to be found.

Dina turned to Andy Murray, a P&G Walmart team alum who had started a small brand design firm, and asked if he could take a crack at the brief and come back with concepts within six days, giving her time to make revisions and present them to Walmart. It was an all-in moment for Andy's agency, and he and his team delivered.

Dina presented the concepts to Walmart and they loved them, but the next step was to figure out how to build them and do a pilot in a couple of stores. And if it worked, which she fully expected, they had to be ready to scale—and quickly.

It was clear to Dina that this was the beginning of something new and not a small request. She would need to acquire the proper brand management resources from Cincinnati and help streamline cash flow to Andy's agency so he could scale a team to grow and execute, not just for the baby department project but potentially for all P&G categories.

Through conversations and negotiations with Deb Henretta, president of P&G's diaper business, Dina secured a brand manager to join the team for a short period as a test. In addition, she and I made the trek to Cincinnati to ask CEO John Pepper for an initial budget of $5 million to test and learn. This was a significant budget for a test, but John approved it.

By working with P&G's purchasing department, Dina found a way to pay Andy's agency, then known as Brandworks, in advance to help provide the cash flow it needed to scale and execute these large programs. With that, the race was on to build an agency with the capabilities needed to conceptualize and execute full-blown shopper marketing programs that initially would partner with P&G to support new brand launches to create shopper awareness ahead of TV advertising.

The principles of collaboration that drove the larger P&G-Walmart relationship were applied to this new partnership. Trust, transparency, and commitment to work through challenges were at the core of the relationship, along with a number of innovative ways of working to streamline workflows and support a one-company model.

While the agency was ramping up, Dina was making the case to bring more brand manager support to the team. Over the course of the next year, Dina got the support to add brand managers from each of the nine core business units. In addition, she built a marketing operations function on the team to ensure tight execution. She also added P&G's insight function (consumer and market knowledge) to the local team.

It was clear that John Pepper's seed budget wasn't going to last very long. Dina needed a separate budget for the shopper marketing work, one that couldn't be flipped into off-invoice discounts. So she and I came up with the "customer development fund."

To outline in principle how the fund would be created and how the dollars would be spent, we needed alignment from Walmart at the top on how the funds could be used. Walmart CEO Lee Scott and I signed an agreement that created the ongoing funding model to support the shopper marketing work and ensured it didn't get conflated with trade spend.

From 1998 to 2003 the newly built shopper marketing team on the ground in Fayetteville, alongside what became ThompsonMurray through an early merger to grow scale, developed and delivered a number of game-changing campaigns to support launches for Iams, Swiffer, Prilosec, Tide Pods, and many more new products into Walmart.

Not long after he was named P&G CEO in 2000, A. G. Lafley shared for the first time his view of the importance of reaching shoppers in stores, and his description of "moments of truth" changed the lexicon of marketing.

"Our business is pretty simple," he told employees during a town hall meeting. "The consumer is our boss, and we have to win with her at two moments of truth day in and day out. We face the first moment of truth at the store shelf, when she decides whether to buy a P&G brand or a competitor's. If we win at the first moment of truth, we get a chance to win at the second, which occurs at home when she and her family use our products and decide whether we've kept our brand promise. Only by winning at both moments of truth—consistently, every day—do we earn consumers' loyalty and sustain the company's growth over the short and long term. And, we have to win *both* moments of truth *millions* of times a day in more than 180 countries worldwide."[1]

The new shopper marketing model was working with P&G at Walmart by winning consumers at that first moment of truth, and it became an essential discipline for understanding how to connect with shoppers.

Dina helped make that happen, first with Walmart and later around the world.

In addition to the successful test with the baby department, she worked with the University of Arkansas and Walmart on branding Supercenters and helped develop our collaborative new store opening program with Walmart that I'll discuss in more detail in another chapter.

Julie Walker (part of Dina's team) also spearheaded the "Speaking of Women's Health" campaign.

You might have noticed that Lafley referred to consumers with feminine pronouns, and that's because the bulk of shoppers were, and still are, women. "Speaking of Women's Health" put a focus on the needs and interests of those decision makers on a variety of topics connected to well-being.

We did promotions, put people in stores to hand out information, and created publications they could sign up to receive. It was a huge success for Walmart because it helped extend their focus on their primary shopper, while it led to increased sales of our products in categories like cosmetics and hair care.

Dina returned to Cincinnati in early 2004 as a senior vice president with the responsibility to expand the new shopper marketing discipline globally inside P&G. In 2004, Saatchi & Saatchi acquired ThompsonMurray to form Saatchi & Saatchi X, which replicated the agency model with P&G worldwide. And the P&G partnership with Saatchi & Saatchi X continues to collaborate on innovation that turns shoppers into buyers.

Note

1. A. G. Lafley, *The Game-Changer: How Every Leader Can Drive Everyday Innovation* (New York: Penguin, 2008), 34.

CHAPTER 19

Ski on Two Skis

W hen you are flying down a snow-covered mountain for the first time
and you aren't familiar with the terrain, it pays to stay balanced over
both skis. Otherwise, you'll soon find yourself out of control and going
headfirst into the trees.

When we were building the one-company model, the concept of balance played a key role because our forward momentum and the tyranny
of the urgent often threatened to disrupt our run. Thus, two of the most
important "skis" for our team were known as "Friday payroll" and "invent
the future."

Friday payroll was about creating reliability, consistency, and efficiency in the transactional operations that were involved with getting
products from the manufacturer to the consumer. The invent-the-future
issues were the things that would set us apart from the competition over
the long haul. This was about embracing the unknown.

These ideas were baked into our strategy of creating capability and
capacity: "We will efficiently deliver Friday's payroll with excellence
while creating increased capacity to deliver breakthrough business
results."

The transactional nature of the relationship, however, can be all-
consuming, leaving no time for the innovative work of the future. You'll
never get to a strategic value-added partnership if your only focus is to
perfect the transactional front. And you won't have a business if all your
time is spent only on innovation. Both have to happen concurrently.

If we overfocused on Friday payroll, eventually the competition would
zip past us like Lindsey Vonn going by gates during an alpine Super G.
On the other hand, if all we did was work on inventing the future, we'd
end up bankrupt before we got off the ski lift.

One example of a Friday payroll issue involved Walmart's practice
of "comping." If a competitor promoted an item at a lower-than-normal

price, Walmart would match that price even if it meant they lost money on each item sold. The competitor's promotion typically lasted a week or two, and then it raised its price back up—usually above Walmart's everyday low price. So it was really important for Walmart to then raise their price back to normal.

Given all the other priorities in a store, however, this was something that could easily be overlooked. And as I mentioned in chapter 16, the longer a "comped" price went uncorrected, the greater the drain on profitability. It also reduced the profit margins for P&G on any of the comped items that we had sold to Walmart.

Eventually, the poor numbers would surface on reports that would lead to discussions and disagreements between P&G's managers and Walmart's buyers and merchandising team.

Mike Graen and his information technology team realized the power of Walmart's data, and, especially with the development of Retail Link, that data now could be analyzed for every product by store and by time period. To make this data actionable, they created several templates, and one of those showed where prices were not being raised back to their normal price.

At the time, six or seven members of P&G's newly created operations team were assigned to various Walmart divisional vice presidents of operations, and we were able to provide them with the comping analysis of stores in their districts and regions. This resulted in much faster compliance when it came to correcting prices and restoring profitability.

Mike's team would also point out opportunities for Walmart to add higher-profit P&G products that they weren't offering. They noted, for instance, that Walmart typically gave prominent displays to our best-selling diaper brand but sold them at a significant loss to help entice shoppers into their stores. The data showed that by adding other P&G diaper options to their mix and pricing them competitively, they could actually increase their overall profit margins.

At the same time, there were also invent-the-future opportunities with the operations teams. For instance, regional or district managers sometimes would recognize ways they might go above and beyond the merchandising plans that came from the home office. So we developed a program that made several promotions available each quarter to operations that went beyond what the buyers at Walmart were making available to them.

Typically, these were things like prebuilt displays or promotions designed to capitalize on a certain demographic, and we made these available three to four months in advance so they could provide us with a firm order and we could produce what they needed.

It was a very clever system of working together to build business, and those initiatives typically went under the radar of their competition and ours because they weren't advertised in the newspaper or on the radio or TV; they were activated in the stores and designed to increase their sales.

During my tenure as team leader, we emphasized the importance of skiing on these two skis—Friday payroll and invent the future. The danger was that as the relationship progressed and we got comfortable on the slopes, we would lean too far on one ski or the other. But we could never take for granted the need for balance, and so there were two questions I almost always asked of team members when I visited with them during the day: What are you working on that involves Friday payroll? And what are you working on to invent the future? We wanted everyone to maintain a dual focus on those strategies.

The best way to invent the future is to do it collaboratively with a strategic partner somewhere in your value chain, and that's what we were doing with Walmart. And the same is true with Friday payroll. Working together on the transactional portions of the relationship allows you to create models that result in reliable, consistent outcomes that benefit both parties.

PART V

A Promise Made Is a Promise Kept

The relentless effort to keep the promises you make is the driving force for any strategic collaboration, and it was central to P&G's transformative relationship with Walmart. This was a bedrock operating principle inside the P&G team. Ultimately, the one-company model worked because Walmart and P&G kept the promises we made to each other. Our promise to each other from the beginning was to create a new way of doing retail partnerships—to disrupt the industry and not just the relationship between P&G and Walmart. And by keeping our promises each day, we kept that bigger promise as well.

CHAPTER 20

The Payoff of Trust

The more success we had with the one-company model, the more momentum we created and the more we developed the type of trust that resulted in fast-paced, almost organic efforts to help improve the other partner's business.

This began with training so that we had a better understanding of each other's business, but it led to more practical ways of helping each other. Our initial efforts to share operational insights led to several examples where trust blossomed into fruitful business.

Good, Better, Best

We realized pretty quickly in our new relationship with Walmart that we had large gaps in our understanding of how retailing worked. So, with Walmart's assistance, we developed a program where all of our new team members spent time working in roles throughout a Walmart store— from receiving stock at night to stocking shelves to working at the front registers.

For the first few years, Walmart also allowed us to participate in the Walton Institute, a weeklong program for their first-level management. This demonstrated our interest in learning more about their business and gave us their vocabulary for better communication. And to reciprocate, P&G invited several senior executives at Walmart to our brand management seminars, which allowed them to see what we considered when developing, managing, and growing our brands.

There were concerns within P&G that Walmart's executives would use what they learned to develop private-label products. But they were going to develop private-label products whether or not they came to our training sessions, so why not help them understand the market and the opportunities for selling private labels along with national brands?

The technology involved in P&G brands could not be easily replicated in a private label, so for the most part Walmart would settle for less effective products, even if they were at a substantially reduced price. By working as partners, we could develop strategies that were complementary rather than competitive.

And, as it turned out, one of the unexpected results of all this cross-training was that P&G learned a great deal from Walmart about what we jointly began calling their "good, better, best" product assortment strategy.

When Walmart began showing us their sales in a category, ranking products based on cost and performance, it was clear that shoppers fell into three price and performance segments. The entry price point in the category was good, and then shoppers could buy a better product for an increase in price and the best product, if one was available in the category, for an additional price premium.

P&G generally sold only premium products—the best in their categories. In a few categories, we also had what would be considered "better," but we typically didn't offer anything at the entry price point. We were all about premium products that would improve the lives of the world's consumers, and that was the way we looked at every product category.

Walmart's approach demonstrated that when the price gap between P&G brands and other brands grew because of their additional price reduction, those brands were able to make market share inroads. If the price gap between their price and P&G's price was too appealing, they would increase their market share at P&G's expense. If a lower-priced brand made too much of an inroad, we would combat that with increased promotional spending to reduce the price gap and build back our market share.

So Walmart recommended that we add products at lower price points, thereby competing with cheaper brands while protecting the profitability of our premium brands. This would prevent us from having to reduce the price, revenue, and profitability of our better and best brands. And as we made product improvements with our best brands, we could transfer improvements to the better brands but at a cheaper price because we now had a new best brand.

P&G began to rethink our positioning in a number of categories. In hair care, for instance, we ended up competing in all three segments—

good, better, and best. But other categories were slower to embrace this approach.

As a team, we made very detailed recommendations, category by category, of what we thought we should do to enter the better category and, in some categories, slightly above good but at a very aggressive price point. That way we protected our innovations and did not allow the competition to erode those benefits.

We sent the recommendations to the leaders of all the categories for introducing new items like Tide Basic, Bounty Basic, and Charmin Basic that would use the same brand name at a lower price point. Those ideas weren't well received at the time, but today P&G offers Simply Tide, Bounty Basic, and Charmin Basic, as well as lower-priced options in several other categories. So while P&G took advantage of the idea at the time, we didn't go all the way until much later.

On the flip side, we helped Walmart understand that while it was important to have the entry price point in a category, they would increase sales and profits if shoppers traded up to better and best products. Walmart saw the wisdom in the trade-up strategy, so while ensuring that they had a very aggressively priced entry-point brand in each category, they promoted in-store displays with more of the better and best brands at their everyday low price to lure shoppers to trade up to the more profitable brands.

The one-company model opened the doors for Walmart to share an opportunity by giving us data that we could use to better understand the market dynamics. And even though we didn't always offer products in the good or better categories, we knew those were important to consumers. We encouraged Walmart to offer all three. In our view, consumers who shopped for good or better often bought at better or best. Then they left the stores with an appreciation for having alternatives that allowed them to make their own decisions.

Dr. John's SpinBrush

Another way Walmart helped P&G was by telling us about John Osher, an entrepreneurial toymaker who came up with a battery-operated toothbrush that he marketed as "Dr. John's SpinBrush."

As his business continued to grow with Walmart, they shared information about the profitability of this low-cost, mechanical toothbrush that children really liked and therefore used to improve their oral health. P&G was so impressed with the product that we bought the company.

The product helped improve sales of Crest while revolutionizing toothbrushes by transforming them from just a simple tool into one that was sold at a higher price point, more profitable to the retailer and to the manufacturer, and a delight to the consumer.

Top to Top

When Walmart wanted to reorganize one of its internal departments, we invited CEO Mike Duke to Cincinnati to visit with our leaders in that area. They shared everything about how our department was organized and answered his questions, which provided valuable input into the decisions he was making.

Additionally, when Walmart decided to develop a lobbying presence in Washington, DC, P&G hosted their leaders to help them understand how P&G organized our efforts. We also introduced them to a number of other resources we had in Washington that proved helpful to them in setting up their operation.

Helping Hands

One other area in which P&G and Walmart began working more closely together was disaster relief efforts.

When there was a hurricane or a tornado or some other event that required a quick response to help those who were affected, Walmart would volunteer their transportation network and P&G would donate products. Walmart trucks would show up at a P&G plant and pick up a load of diapers or cleaning products, for instance, and ensure that it got to the right place to help the people who needed it.

As Walmart grew, its ability to help at scale also grew. And with that growth came new opportunities and challenges for our partnership.

CHAPTER 21

Expanding the Model

A fter the successful first year, the one-company model received the stamp of approval from P&G CEO John Smale. Customer business development (CBD) became part of the new way P&G did business, and the approach rapidly took root and began to spread.

Mike Milligan, a senior vice president at P&G and one of my mentors, became the global head of CBD and was charged with evaluating the potential of expanding the concept to our other retail customers—including competitors of Walmart.

Mike was perfect for that role. He had a background in sales and as vice president of the food product division, and he was as tough as nails in his expectation of those who worked for him. Importantly, he had little patience for P&G's internal resistance to change.

Under Mike's leadership, we developed a process for determining which other retail customers were suited for the CBD teams. It wasn't like we were inviting every retailer to the P&G barbershop and offering a nice haircut. They had to be a good strategic fit, the size of the prize had to be worth the investment, there had to be a cultural fit between the two companies, and there had to be a strong commitment, particularly on the side of the retailer, to devote the resources and the time needed to make it work.

Mike and I started having discussions with senior-level executives from other retailers, including Kmart, Target, and Costco, to see if they were interested in this new approach and to lay out the requirements and expectations for these relationships.

Our intent wasn't to replicate what was done in the relationship with Walmart but to better understand each customer's strategy and then assess how P&G brands and capabilities could help them achieve their goals while moving the P&G business forward at the same time.

We developed assessments and codesigned processes with these customers, and over a period of about a year we formally established CBD teams for each of them. Interestingly, the Walmart team was the only one where the leader (me) actually moved to the site of the customer's headquarters. The leaders of the three other teams (who all had previously worked for me) remained in Cincinnati, while their teams relocated to the cities where the retailers were based.

The expansion of CBD teams worked well for the customers and for P&G, and several years later we expanded the concept to grocery retailers like Kroger. Then I began traveling around the world to share the concept with the leading retailers in the United Kingdom, France, Germany, Spain, Portugal, Japan, Italy, and Australia.

Members of my leadership team and I also met with the P&G business leaders in those countries to help them understand the benefits and expectations. It was important for both parties to know the time and monetary investment required to achieve success with the one-company model. There was no magic switch to do so; rather it took a collaborative commitment to designing and implementing the new structure and practices that would make it work.

Since Walmart didn't have a concrete plan for international expansion at that time, they had no problem with P&G expanding the model into new markets. The retailers in other countries, meanwhile, were cautious but eventually receptive to the change.

With Tesco in the United Kingdom, for instance, we presented the concept to CEO Terry Leahy, and he was intrigued enough that he asked me to present the concept and answer questions with his leadership team.

Initially, there was considerable skepticism. John Molter, whom you might remember as the guy on our original design team who had cornflakes for his "proper English breakfast" on our way out of Arkansas, now was coordinating the P&G business with Tesco, and he suggested that the Tesco leaders come to the United States and see for themselves that we weren't selling a "smoke and mirrors" scheme.

Mike Milligan and I agreed, so long as John wasn't in charge of breakfast. A few weeks later we hosted a multifunctional group of leaders from Tesco that was headed by Terry's top lieutenant, John Gildersleeve. They spent a week experiencing the concept from soup to nuts. The highlight of their trip was when Walmart's senior officers hosted them for an afternoon at our request and sang praises about the benefits they were deriving from the approach with P&G.

As a result of the trip, P&G and Tesco agreed to replicate the process that we used with Walmart. With John Molter as the P&G team leader, the relationship blossomed and provided enormous benefits for both companies.

Once Tesco started to see and experience the benefits, they expanded and took a more collaborative approach with their fresh suppliers, like those for eggs and milk, and together they had some amazing breakthroughs in increased sales and more cost-effective ways of handling and replenishing those products.

As interest in the concept grew internationally, our team designed a weeklong training and development seminar for P&G team leaders in other countries that included presentations and tips for every function and on multiple levels. Our multifunctional leadership team also served as consultants to the P&G functions as they ramped up their version of the Walmart Customer Team with their retailers.

Suppliers Take Notice

The concept of more formal collaboration was quite appealing to many of our retail customers, as well as to our competitors. Once the P&G relationship with Walmart became broadly publicized in newspapers and magazines, other consumer product companies went to Walmart to see if it was something they should do as well.

Walmart made it clear that it was not a new requirement for their suppliers to have an office in the Bentonville area, but they also said they were open to improved relationships with suppliers based on what they had learned and were experiencing with P&G.

Many consumer packaged goods (CPG) companies, of course, don't compete directly with P&G. Our leadership team spent time with senior executives from Rubbermaid, for instance, to review what we were doing and how we were making it work.

Gradually one company after another established a presence in Northwest Arkansas and put resources on the ground. The level and number of people varied based on the discussions with Walmart and capabilities that they wanted to put on the team.

For Walmart, the relationship with P&G was beneficial to their relationship with other CPG companies because we were creating and cocreating templates that their other partners could use but without threatening us.

We developed ways to use data from Retail Link, for instance, to develop more strategic approaches for distributing P&G products in each geographic region and every store. Other CPG companies could use these types of templates with Walmart, but they still had to invest the resources and time to bring the data to life so that it would help them make better decisions. Some made the most of the data; others didn't.

As other CPG companies had success with Walmart and saw that P&G was expanding with Kmart, Target, and Costco, they also began discussions with those retailers. And, in many cases, they put teams in place with those customers as well.

Looking over the landscape of these expansions to other CPG companies, we saw varying degrees of success largely based on how well the supplier dealt with internal issues. Often their senior management was not totally aligned, committed, and willing to make the changes necessary. Or they weren't able to identify the right resources and have the right business processes inside their company that would support a team on the ground in Northwest Arkansas.

We had a competitive advantage because we had a head start as the originators of the idea and because P&G was such a well-resourced expert in the industry. We kept inventing, testing, and experimenting to ensure we stayed in the lead. We even had sweatshirts made that featured a dogsled team and the phrase, "Unless you are the lead dog, the view never changes!"

At the same time, we had a deep responsibility and obligation not to compromise any of the information or business processes that our customers trusted us with since a higher level of data was being shared.

For instance, none of the senior members of the P&G Walmart team could move to any other retail customer without at least a one-year assignment in a corporate role that was not in any way specific to another retailer.

Expanding beyond CPG

As P&G's relationship with Walmart continued to progress, the one-company model began to draw interest from companies in other industries.

The Strategic Account Management Association, whose membership included Boise Cascade, IBM, Xerox, Motorola, Intel, and several large chemical companies, asked me to give a presentation at one of its conferences about the way we were working with Walmart. They later asked me to join the organization representing P&G, and eventually I became its board chairman.

The concept of multifunctional customer teams expanded into other industries with varying degrees of success, and, again, it was based on the commitment from each company, the commitment from the top, and willingness to put the appropriate resources and processes together to make them work for their customers.

Their results were also influenced by how receptive their customers were to the new way of working. Collaborative relationships require a commitment from both companies, and if that doesn't happen, the chances of success are not very good.

I found it interesting that a number of the other industries already had global relationships with their customers, but they weren't well coordinated across geographies. P&G grew globally with the Walmart relationship in a very coordinated manner, and that sparked additional interest in how companies could develop and execute a global strategy with their customers.

The success of the one-company model also gave rise to a few individuals and consulting teams that have pushed forward with new tools that guide companies through the collaborative process, including two individuals in Switzerland whom I coached and mentored over an extended period, Michael Weller and Christoph Senn.

Michael has built and led successful multifunctional relationships between two global supplier companies and their global customers. He did that at DSM, a science-based company that sells health and nutritional ingredients to large companies such as Nestlé, Bayer, and Aptar, a packaging company.

His leadership demonstrated the ability for smaller, specialty companies to become strategic suppliers to their much larger suppliers. Michael also started a consultancy to help teach companies how to partner. His company was called Connect to Win, which was very appropriate.

Christoph is an adjunct professor at INSEAD and the founder and chairman of Valuecreator, which helps organizations create value by fostering high-value relationships. He has a detailed process supported by a replica of our model and has developed proprietary software and coaching.

CHAPTER 22

The Triune Mandate

The one-company model took off because we pursued several opportunities that had been lurking in the background of the retail industry for decades. But it soared, in my opinion, because we also adapted to a rapid succession of change during those early years.

Both companies learned from the relationship, and we used that understanding to help each other grow in three high-change areas—retail formats, categories, and geography. I refer to this as our "triune mandate" because all three areas were growing at a fast rate and at the same time, so they were simultaneously high priorities. You couldn't even label them 1a, 1b, and 1c—they were all number one.

To maximize our efficiency and make the most of what we learned, we developed a robust reapplication program when it came to categories, countries, and formats.

We took whatever worked in one situation and looked for opportunities to expand it into other situations. This allowed us to move fast (based on known results and investment cost) while creating a competitive advantage by advancing in ways that frequently were hidden from competitors until changes hit the market.

Retail Formats

Walmart constantly changed the prototypes for its stores—things like the layout or the size of various departments—and, of course, they tested totally new formats along the way.

Some ideas didn't work. The 213,000-square-foot Hypermart that opened in 1987 in Garland, Texas, and was the first of the four giant, offer-everything mall-like stores with associates roller-skating (and falling) in the massive aisles had some short-term success but was only marginally profitable.

"Our Hypermarts weren't disasters," Sam Walton would write, "but they were disappointments."[1]

Walmart took what it learned from that experiment, as it did with most experiments, and used the lessons to create other, more sustainable formats.

The most successful new formats were Sam's Club, which launched in 1983; the Supercenter, which rose from the Hypermart's ashes in 1988 and made Walmart competitive in the grocery business; and the Neighborhood Market, which first opened in 1998. Walmart created Walmart.com in 2000 and, after a slow start, eventually made e-commerce a profitable part of their business.

For P&G, the growth of new formats required more staffing, so our team got bigger and bigger. We had a Sam's Club team, a Supercenter team, a Neighborhood Market team, and one individual dedicated to online sales.

Because we were multifunctional, these teams shared information about what worked and what might be applied in other areas—something that worked in Sam's Club might, with slight modifications, also work at a Supercenter and Neighborhood Market.

As previously discussed, because we were mining data at the store levels, we were able to share new ideas that were backed with proven results. And by marrying our consumer and market data with their store data, we were able to better customize product assortment in their stores to meet the specific demographics of each geography.

Walmart, meanwhile, used P&G as a resource to explore better ways to market their formats. No one was better than P&G at developing a brand, and we showed them ways to treat each format as a brand and market it more successfully. We even did shopper research for them on Supercenters using University of Arkansas students under the supervision of our consumer and market knowledge team. This provided them with great feedback on their strengths and areas for improvement.

Categories

As we progressed and offered compelling evidence of the multifunctional team's success, more and more P&G category general managers jumped on board. We were able to design and staff more strategically, and we soon built teams that were totally focused on each P&G category. They were in Arkansas as part of our team, but also part of the category team in Cincinnati.

The partnership also fueled P&G's growth into entirely new categories with brands like Swiffer, Febreze, Prilosec, and Pūr. Walmart actually worked with us to design the launch plans and then lead in the execution of those plans.

The Swiffer brand, for example, required a different shelving system and a unique location in the store, as well as an unusual launch when it debuted in 1999.

Swiffer basically took away the bucket, mop, broom, and dustpan, and reinvented the entire cleaning category. Instead of having a one-time purchase of items at fairly low prices and low margins, this was more akin to the razor and the razorblade category with considerably higher prices, repeat sales, and increased profits. If P&G could get the units in homes, consumers would buy buckets of the refill products.

Walmart spent a lot of time with the P&G team, determining what these products would look like in stores and what issues we would face as the category moved forward. This really helped P&G tighten up what turned out to be one of the most exemplary launches of a new category in the industry. Just consider how many changes were required in a store to create this new space and the fact that it had to be done partly on faith and trust.

Walmart has been a participant and beneficiary in the brands' long-term growth because they invested in the development from the beginning.

Geography

In 1980, Walmart operated 276 stores that were mostly in the central part of the United States. By 1992, the year Sam Walton died, Walmart had 1,928 stores and clubs, including a Sam's Club that opened in 1991 in Mexico City. They purchased 122 Woolco stores in Canada and expanded north in 1994 and opened their first store in China in 1996.

This type of rapid expansion represented tremendous opportunities for P&G to grow our business but also to partner with Walmart in ways that helped them succeed.

For instance, we worked with Walmart to create a new store opening plan that built on Sam's tradition of creating tremendous fanfare when entering a new market. The plan included things like entertainment for shoppers, information on navigating the store, and, of course, merchandising promotions that involved a number of the P&G brands.

Our shopper marketing agency (ThompsonMurray, which later became Saatchi & Saatchi X) helped us create this plan, and we partnered with a few other suppliers that weren't our competitors (meat producers and Coca-Cola, for instance). With five or six participants, we could spread out the costs of welcoming shoppers to the new store and offer a variety of product samples.

This was so successful that we used it as a blueprint for Walmart's new store openings in Canada, including the Woolco stores they acquired and converted, and as they opened new stores and clubs around the world.

Our work with Saatchi & Saatchi X on in-store promotions (like the Baby Centers) also was easy to replicate in other markets, foreign and domestic. We often developed something for the United States, Canada, or Mexico and then offered it in other countries. We had paid for the idea in the original market, so our teams in other countries were able to have a tested, successful promotion that they wouldn't have been able to afford on their own. It also gave them something their competition didn't see coming because they weren't wired to look for it.

These promotions helped not only P&G and Walmart but Saatchi & Saatchi X. They entered new markets with their P&G business, and then offered their innovative shopper marketing concepts to other clients as well.

Uniquely Positioned

P&G was uniquely positioned to partner with Walmart in several ways with its international expansion, because we were already a global company with years of experience in markets outside the United States.

When Sam and his son, Rob Walton, were considering the partnership that led to their expansion in Mexico, for instance, we provided marketplace information based on our business there and a list of bankers, lawyers, real estate brokers, government officials, and other key contacts from our working relationships.

We also hosted a dinner for Walmart executives with the top consumer products companies in Mexico. Sam presented his vision, solic-
ited support, and responded to questions from these suppliers, while we
described our relationship with Walmart.

A few years later when Walmart was considering its expansion into
China, P&G CEO John Pepper met with Rob Walton to discuss the mer-
its of the idea. John had been a champion of P&G's expansion in China, so
he shared what we had learned and what we believed about the market's
potential.

As Walmart expanded internationally, I made it a point to attend all
the grand openings for their first store in a new market and often for new
product launches. I not only supported our team in that country, but my
presence sent an important message to the senior leaders from Walmart
who were there about P&G's commitment to the one-company model.

Andy Jett, the first head of international for our P&G team, and I often
traveled to Walmart's newest markets, visited different stores, took pictures of things Walmart's competitors were doing, and noted things that
were impressive or were opportunities for them. And when we learned
about new countries that were on Walmart's expansion list, we traveled
there and provided Walmart with a market analysis and anything else
that might be helpful.

Mexico, of course, came first and provided the foundations for all that
followed in our international efforts with Walmart.

After Walmart struck a deal with Cifra, a Mexican retailer, and began
planning and opening stores and clubs south of the border, our multifunctional P&G team in Fayetteville began working with P&G Mexico to support the necessary programs and changes to support Walmart's expansion.

Eventually, we had an entire multifunctional team in Mexico that
reported to the local country but with strong dotted lines back to the
P&G team in Fayetteville. We developed the talent in Mexico to take
greater and greater responsibility for leading the business but always with
a link to the Fayetteville mothership.

Each time Walmart entered a new country, we established a working
relationship with the local P&G organization and expanded our team so
that we had two representatives dedicated to Walmart on the ground.
And each of the functional representatives on that team had a connection
with the functional head on our team in Fayetteville.

We followed this model as Walmart expanded into Canada, Argentina, Brazil, China, Korea, Indonesia, Germany, and the United Kingdom. In fact, we developed a plug-and-play process for every function and every format that Walmart would introduce into a country.

The new structure, however, caused some initial tension. The requirements we needed to implement in each of these countries frequently cut across the priorities or budgets of the individual countries. And members of the team in a new country were now connected to our team in Fayetteville, while also reporting to the management in their country. We resolved the conflicts over time by consistently demonstrating the value of our approach.

The new arrangement benefited P&G in the country where Walmart expanded in several ways. We helped each of these subsidiaries modernize their systems to meet Walmart's needs, for instance, by setting them up with electronic data interchange and Retail Link. This gave us a huge advantage over our competitors. We knew Walmart's success would prompt other retailers to imitate their approach, and we already would have systems in place to support them.

We also provided training and development opportunities for team members in these countries, and our leadership would conduct seminars to help them improve.

Some members of those teams took international assignments by coming to Fayetteville to work on our team, and team members from Fayetteville frequently moved to other countries.

Henry Ho, for instance, came to Arkansas as a logistics specialist and later spent nearly six years in Hong Kong leading our international team there.

Tom Verdery, who started in sales, was our first international team leader, carrying our culture and vision to Mexico. And when Tom left, Rich Kley, who started as an analyst, took the team lead in Mexico.

"I got to take what I learned on the Walmart team to Mexico, Switzerland, Poland, then outside of P&G," Rich told me.[2]

Mark Breden went from having a sales role to leading our Argentina team, Pete Silvestri moved from an operations role in the United States to a leadership role on the Puerto Rico team, Tom McDonald led the initial team in the United Kingdom, and Eugene Dubejsky led the team in Canada.

The Canadian startup was a tremendous success as Eugene and Walmart vice president Brent Berry (an original mirror team member) worked seamlessly to deploy in rapid succession every idea that had worked in another market. The result was that Walmart quickly became the destination store for P&G products.

For Walmart, having a P&G team in each of their countries and having those teams connected to the US team was a huge advantage. It helped them get their programs implemented quickly and gave them leverage with other suppliers.

Early on, Walmart based its international division in Bentonville while also having a team in each country. Since we were uniquely staffed to work with Walmart's global group, we attended and gave presentations when they had meetings for their international people and helped them brainstorm and quickly implement new ideas.

Also, once we developed templates for using Retail Link to analyze categories and markets and knew what to look for in all that data, we provided that expertise to our teams in each country. This gave them a huge advantage over competitors who managed their Walmart business separately in each country.

Going to China

Expanding to China, as John Pepper told Rob Walton, came with challenges and opportunities for Walmart. With billions of potential customers, the upsides were obvious, but every culture is different, and the geopolitical issues were (and still are) trickier with China than almost any other market.

Not only was P&G able to provide Walmart with insights into these dynamics, but we became an ongoing partner with them once they entered the market.

For starters, our team added Andy Jett, one of the original team members who helped P&G open our business in China. He spoke flawless Mandarin and Cantonese and had lived in China while on multiple assignments, so he was a great resource to Walmart and P&G in building a successful partnership around this new business.

Another key player was Joe Hatfield, one of Walmart's early leaders in its expansion into China. Joe had made up his mind that he was going to be the Sam Walton of Walmart in China, and the care that he had for his associates and the examples that he set in terms of work ethic and standards were amazing. Over and over we saw examples of this, like Joe helping build a store display with associates as he taught them and mentored them.

The biggest challenge we faced on our team when Walmart expanded to China was getting funding to create a team there. I went to Dimitri Panayotopoulos, the president of P&G China, and asked for three or four dedicated resources who would support the Walmart startup and ensure that the technology infrastructure we needed would be in place.

Dimitri, a good friend and a very good businessman, wasn't buying what I was selling, and not without good reason.

"Tom, I love you," he told me, "but I would be crazy if I gave you dedicated resources to support three or four stores when I don't have the resources I need to support our own expansion in China. If I gave you those resources, I would have a mutiny among my leadership team. I understand the importance of Walmart to P&G's overall business, but there's nothing I can do to support that."

Disappointed but undeterred, I went to John Pepper and told him our P&G policies were forcing us to make a very bad decision when it came to supporting Walmart's expansion into China. As always, he listened patiently to my point of view and asked probing questions. Then he agreed that I was right to ask for the resources and that Dimitri was right in his decision to protect his budget.

As we discussed an acceptable solution, I suggested that he make a two-year loan from his discretionary budget to pay for the personnel we needed there. They would not only support Walmart's expansion into China but provide a huge resource to P&G China by helping them get ready to win with the modern trade that eventually would follow Walmart's success there. I also told him we would help in the development of P&G China people by including them in any seminars and any other training sessions we offered.

John's decision to provide those resources for two years jump-started our business there, and we never looked back.

Notes

1. Sam Walton, *Sam Walton: Made in America* (New York: Random House, 2012), Kindle edition, 254.
2. Rich Kley, interview with the author, 2023.

CHAPTER 23

Seasons of Change

T he Bible tells us that when God created the world, he paused at the end of each day's work and pronounced it "good." However, he didn't say it was finished. Later he would talk about things being "finished," but that's an entirely different story.

My point here is that just because you create something with intentionality, even something as awe inspiring and indescribable as the universe, that doesn't necessarily mean it's finished. Indeed, creation typically is just the beginning—the genesis, if you will.

The genesis of the one-company model was never intended to be a one-and-done creation. Our job was to establish the foundations and the structures that would create success and momentum and then, with ongoing care and innovation, carry the relationship between Walmart and P&G far into the future.

The original P&G-Walmart team created a unique type of jigsaw puzzle. We came up with pieces of a vision, then we moved them around until we got them all in the right place to make the picture. But we were willing to shake up the pieces, add new pieces, and remove others to create new pictures that were more relevant to the changing environment along the way.

The puzzle took many different forms, but it was never finished. There was always a fresh and better version waiting for the next iterative creation. But is that still the case? Is this puzzle destined for a tattered box on the back of the shelf of a game room? Or is the one-company model still relevant?

Those are questions worthy of an answer.

To Everything There Is a Season

Scripture also tells us about the reality of seasons in life. There's a season for everything. Seasons change. And nothing under the sun lasts forever.

This is such a universal reality that in 1959 it jumped from the pages of Ecclesiastes to the airways of popular radio when Peter Seeger penned "Turn! Turn! Turn!," also known as "To Everything There Is a Season."[1]

Sam Walton and Lou Pritchett kicked off a new season in business relationships when they went on that famous canoe trip in 1987 on the Spring River. The conditions and timing were right for a new approach. It was a season for planting new fields, a season of change. And, as I've tried to demonstrate, things changed radically! Those fields created incredible growth, and the harvest, for thirty-plus years, has been bountiful.

The world continues to change, and so must any approach to collaborative partnerships. We all are works in progress. The conditions are not the same as during that initial season of collaboration. The market has been reshaped by new players, especially Amazon, and advancements in technology. And it's been rocked by the influence of an unprecedented pandemic.

Walmart, of course, is a very different company from what it was in the 1980s or 1990s. It is an omni-channel, multinational retailer that continues to innovate with technology and with new ways to reach consumers. It has around 2.1 million associates. It operates more than ten thousand stores in nineteen countries. And its revenue in fiscal year 2023 was roughly $164 billion.

The larger Walmart has grown, unfortunately, the greater the challenge for maintaining close relationships with even their biggest suppliers. By necessity, Walmart has brought in more and more senior leaders from other companies. These external hires have been tremendous additions by providing much-needed expertise and skills in areas Walmart needed to maintain its competitive position, but it takes time for new associates to adapt to the company's culture or to familiarize themselves with the relationships and processes that helped make a partnership successful.

The number of consumer packaged goods companies that now have teams in Northwest Arkansas, meanwhile, makes it much harder for Walmart to interact in a special way with all of them—or even some of them. And these teams have their own struggles with turnover. As people leave or move from one company to another, continuity inevitably suffers.

These all are factors that have added complexity to the relationships between suppliers and retailers. But that doesn't mean this approach is somehow less relevant than it was in the late 1980s and early 1990s when it all began. It just means it's different.

The Next Seasons of Change

Much of my time in the years since I retired from P&G has been spent visiting with CEOs and their leadership teams and consulting with companies about how they might rethink their relationship with their customers, suppliers, or both.

None of them, I can tell you, have needed exactly what P&G and Walmart created. As I often tell them, there's no one-size solution to creating a collaborative partnership. You have to approach it like you are buying a tailored suit or dress, not like you're buying a hammer.

There are options for hammers, but one will pretty much do the job just as well as another. If you need to pound a nail, buy a quality hammer and pound away. But let's say your only daughter is getting married. Or you are an actor or actress headed to an awards show. Or you just want to look great for a night on the town. Any old outfit won't do. You want something that's designed for the occasion and that fits you like it fits no one else. So you go to a dressmaker or tailor, as the case may be.

As any good tailor will tell you, the key is to measure twice and cut once. In other words, you need to figure out what's needed and why, then carefully plan your approach, because choices have consequences. A thorough assessment and analysis can allow any company to determine how tactical and how strategic it needs to be in its approach to partnerships.

Typically, there are three potential paths.

One, a strategic collaboration that's customized for the two companies but modeled after the one-company approach taken by Walmart and P&G.

Two, a collaboration where both companies are committed to adding value to the other, even if they aren't deeply connected by shared strategies.

And three, a transactional partnership where both companies benefit, if only by doing whatever it is they do best but in a way that benefits both companies.

At some level, however, I can assure you that nearly every company is better off working collaboratively with their customers and suppliers to identify and solve the issues that will help both of them grow their business. They just need to set aside their hammers and start making suits and dresses.

The basics of tailoring haven't changed much over the centuries. Tools have changed. Styles have changed. Materials have changed. But many of the same techniques and skills used to make padded linen garments to wear under a suit of armor in the Middle Ages are still used to make a fashionable tuxedo for the Oscars.

In much the same way, the one-company model is still relevant to every business and every industry, not just to suppliers and retailers. Things that have needed to change have changed along the way, but the timeless core values, fundamental best practices, and relevant operating principles are what business leaders need in every season, and especially when it's time to sow and grow the partnerships of the future.

P&G helped show the way in the 1980s and 1990s, and I believe it is well positioned to lead its industry and other industries into this next season.

The key to the original season of change was the commitment by the leaders at the top of the two organizations, and P&G CEO Jon Moeller sees strategic partnerships as a priority in the company's corporate strategy.

"I'm a big believer in strategic partnerships as opposed to transactional partnerships," Jon said in March 2023 during a conference hosted by MIT. And P&G's approach to those partnerships, he said, is to try to "build *our* reality as opposed to your reality and my reality."[2]

The P&G Walmart team in Northwest Arkansas also has the benefit of extraordinary continuity in its leadership—just three global team leaders since 1988. The recognition and reward system that P&G created in the early years allowed people to stay in key roles and add value to the team without sacrificing their career progress, status, and economic rewards. That continuity has helped build and maintain the type of trust that's essential to a highly productive, long-term relationship.

Settlers replaced the pioneers on the team, but P&G has kept the partnership approach relevant by maintaining its commitment to an innovative culture. The saying is true: culture eats strategy for lunch. Without the right culture, the partnership will starve.

A pioneering spirit, especially in a more developed environment, allows for and encourages new ideas and challenges the existing ways of doing business. This type of innovation has come from new team members who have brought fresh perspectives and from everyone working to learn from what has worked and not worked along the way.

And P&G is much faster than it was in the early 1990s when it comes to responding to opportunities, reducing bureaucracy, and empowering contributors in all layers of the organization rather than sticking with the former hierarchical command-and-control model.

Walmart and other major retail players, meanwhile, stand to benefit from a new season of investment in the partnership model.

Despite the changes in the market, Walmart continues to benefit from the work it does in partnership with P&G and from collaborations with many other companies that have access to shared data. This includes major industry players, but also many promising startups that gain access to participate with the world's largest retailer.

In recent years, much of the discussion about partnerships with suppliers has been on sustainability efforts and strengthening the efficiencies and resilience of supply chains. And developing new and better ways to create and take advantage of the partnerships will yield better results for Walmart and for their partners, just as it did when we pioneered change three decades ago.

Regardless of what Walmart and P&G do with the future of their partnership, other businesses need to emphasize collaboration, not only with each other but with academics. One of the most fruitful partnerships for P&G during my time (and more so today) was with business schools like the one at the University of Arkansas. Industry and academia need to work together to advance theory, but also to develop technologies and best practices.

At the UA's Sam M. Walton College of Business, for instance, industry leaders coauthor research papers with faculty, provide data for research and for use in classes, lecture in classes, teach classes, serve on panels, mentor students, take part in executive education, provide case studies, and, of course, hire students for internships and full-time jobs.

No matter what type of partnership is needed between organizations, however, the essentials are the same: commitment at the top to a worthwhile vision, an innovation-oriented culture, rewards and recognition systems that honor those doing the work, and a creative and persistent mindset for finding opportunities and developing solutions.

These things never go out of style, but they don't happen on their own. They need a good tailor. Or a good farmer. Pick your metaphor. Plant, cultivate, and harvest. Measure twice, cut once, and carefully stitch it together. Heck, pick both metaphors. You and your business partners will look great and eat well. Everybody wins.

Notes

1. Ecclesiastes 3:1–8.
2. Dylan Walsh, "Procter & Gamble's CEO on Navigating Rapid Change," MIT Sloan School of Management, May 2, 2023, https://mitsloan.mit.edu/ideas-made-to-matter/procter-gambles-ceo-navigating-rapid-change.

Epilogue

My Long Walk to Change

In *The Long Walk to Freedom*, Nelson Mandela, the former dissident turned prime minister, wrote, "There is nothing like returning to a place that remains unchanged to find the ways in which you yourself have altered."[1]

Unlike Mandela, when I return to the story of the one-company model, I see a landscape that has changed dramatically. I see collaborative disruptions everywhere I look. But much like Mandela, the greatest changes, and perhaps the hardest to make, were with myself. At the outset, I mentioned that this story isn't about me, but I also pointed out that the experience changed me, and perhaps there's something to be learned from a quick look at my personal transformation.

I stepped into the role of team leader for the experiment with Walmart eager to change the world, or at least my part of it. But I had no idea what the next several years would bring and the personal improvements I would need to make to broaden my skills to give us all a shot at success.

We were dealing with a multifunctional team in a complex environment, and I was forced to play on a bigger stage with higher stakes and more adversity than in any of my previous roles.

I needed to expand my thinking about the role I would play as a general manager and the skills I would need to understand all the different functions, how they fit together, and how to equip and motivate the people involved—not just those who reported to me, but everyone else who in some way made decisions or took actions that played a role in our success.

The more I've reflected on this adventure, the more I've seen "communicator" as my most important role. I was the communicator of the vision, of the culture, and of the result, and I communicated those things throughout Walmart and P&G and to other retailers and suppliers, to universities, and to industries.

I learned, for instance, how to listen with curiosity rather than listening while focusing on what I already knew (or thought I knew). The old saying is true: what you don't know won't hurt you as much as what you know that ain't so. Nothing is as harmful as faulty assumptions.

I had strong opinions on many things or often believed things operated in one way or another, but by developing my ability to listen and ask questions, I was better able to understand the reality we were dealing with and the options that were available. I found better ways to deal with conflicting opinions, grew more effective in persuasion, and became less apt to force round pegs into square holes.

The ability to effectively communicate up, down, and sideways to a variety of audiences was instrumental in any success that we had.

We were dealing with an environment at P&G that involved all different levels, all different functions, and all the different product divisions. We were dealing with Walmart at all of its different functions, levels, and business units. And we were dealing with a team that had a variety of experiences and came from several different functions and backgrounds.

In my case, I had to learn how to present to a board of directors at both Walmart and P&G, as well as to all types of senior executives. And I'll reluctantly concede to Mike Graen that this eventually included giving up the overhead projector for PowerPoint slides.

I also had to improve my verbal communication skills in formal and informal settings, with groups, and with individuals, and I had to improve my writing skills, because we quickly determined that we needed an agreed-on and recorded history if we were going to be successful for the long term. That was the only way that people would be able to build on each other's success.

Those who worked with me would likely agree that my strengths set me up for success as a leader. I was very energetic and hardworking, and I had high standards for myself and those who worked with and for me. I was creative but also driven by results, so driven that I was fearless in the face of adversity. And my loyalty to my team resulted in a commitment to giving them credit and to helping them develop professionally and personally.

At times, however, I overplayed those strengths, and I had what all would agree were some rough edges. I didn't always fully understand the risk and consequences, for instance, when I fearlessly took on our adversaries. I could easily get to the boiling point when challenged, unleashing what I would sometimes refer to as my "Italian animation."

I could be harshly critical of those who didn't see things my way, and I offered little grace for performances that didn't meet my expectations. Though I was loyal to my team, I also could be overly protective and defensive of them while perhaps discounting the legitimate ideas and opinions of those who weren't on our team. I drove people too hard, wasn't always a good or patient listener, and too often moved too quickly to action.

My team, my mentors, and even some of my adversaries, however, helped me grow as a servant leader. They were collaborators in my personal disruption.

There are many good definitions and descriptions of servant leadership, but I always liked the "head, heart, and hands" model that we learned in our work with John Brown University.

The head was where you needed to have information, knowledge, and rationale of the principles.

Then you had to have a heart to really commit to each other and the willingness to be vulnerable to bring the concept to life with the commitment to bring the knowledge into play consistently.

And you also had to use your hands to do the practical things required to make it successful and integrate it into the culture.

One of my mentors, Ken Blanchard, added "habits" to that model. This speaks to consistency in how you and your teams operate to achieve success.

It's one thing to understand the principles of servant leadership, but it's another to put them into practice each and every day. And if I were to point at one way the experience of leading the P&G Walmart team changed me the most, it is that it made me a better servant leader.

Not perfect, Lord knows. But better.

It's a bit counterintuitive, but I believe that transformation took place only because people like Sam Walton, Don Soderquist, Ken Blanchard, Mike Milligan, and John Pepper helped me keep my focus off myself and on my team and our shared success.

John Green, one of our first data analysts, reminded me of this reality when he recalled a conversation we had on a flight during those early days. Somehow the topic landed on what motivated him in his work, and he was telling me about the sense of satisfaction he got when he saw that his analysis resulted in better sales for the company.

That's what motivated him, he said, and I thought that was a great answer. It fit perfectly for his personality and that season of his career. Then he flipped the question.

"What keeps you motivated during the day?" he asked me.

The answer to that was tied to a goal I set for myself early in my career, and it had nothing to do with our business results. Someone had pointed out that most of us can quickly fill a list of the top five most influential people in our lives with the names of a coach, a teacher, relatives, and longtime friends. The next five, however, might expand out and include someone we've worked with. So my goal was to be in the top ten of as many people as possible.

With that in mind, I told John what motivated me.

"I like to watch my people grow," I told him.

What happened when they grew? P&G won. Walmart won. Consumers won. Our other retail customers won. The people on my team won. And I won. We all won. Together.

Note

1. Nelson Mandela, *Long Walk to Freedom* (New York: Little, Brown and Company, 1994), 73.

Vision of the Future

This vision document, drafted in February 1987 by our internal P&G team, painted a remarkably accurate picture of what Walmart and P&G would create.

It is 1992–1993 and business is very good. For the past five years, Wal-Mart and P&G have been working together to achieve a mutually developed "vision of the future." Their cooperative effort has led to the achievement of significantly increased market shares for both companies, supported by volume and profit growth rates well ahead of their competition in Wal-Mart's marketing area. Realization of this vision has resulted from a focus on and continual improvement of their most important jointly owned systems and processes. It is a highly effective and efficient business-building partnership based on common long-term objectives and mutual trust.

Some characteristics of this business relationship are:

1. Both Wal-Mart and P&G work together on the assumption that the business and administrative problems they experience together or separately reflect the existing systems that produce them. Consequently, they know that if they expect to improve upon the output of these systems, they first must understand these systems and then move to change and improve them together.

2. Before either Wal-Mart or P&G moves to make a significant change in systems or procedures which they know will likely affect the other or both companies, they consult each other and gather sufficient data prior to making any decision to change.

3. Administrative work related to the operations of both companies is greatly simplified, requiring only minimum overhead and staffing. The amount of time spent correcting misunderstandings and administrative errors is insignificant.

4. P&G's restructured sales organization has a sharply reduced number of people interfacing with Wal-Mart decision-makers. Moreover, these P&G managers have been delegated significant responsibility to take action on the business-building steps they develop with their Wal-Mart counterparts.

5. P&G's promotion programs have been designed with optimum input from its customers. Importantly, they are appropriately flexible so as to better fit the strategic pricing and merchandising plans of all customers.

6. Wal-Mart's "continuous replenishment system" is being supported efficiently by all P&G divisions. Specifically, orders to P&G for delivery to Wal-Mart's warehouses and direct to stores are made on optimum timing to meet Wal-Mart's requirements. The business-building effect of this continually improving system is such that P&G's distribution costs are either maintained or reduced over time.

7. Wal-Mart and P&G derive maximum operating efficiencies from their cooperative use of uniform communication standards (UCS) and their expanded application of bar code capabilities. All orders and invoicing communications are electronically executed. Product orders are generated automatically as scanning occurs at checkout, and every order is traceable through each distribution channel as a result of scanning applications.

8. Their work together on the collection and analysis of direct product costing (DPC) data has led to greater collaboration on packaging designs for optimum operating efficiencies (e.g., warehouse handling, shelf stocking, etc.). This design work applies to both primary selling units and the secondary containers, which are used to deliver product to warehouses and stores. As a result, P&G's packages and containers are increasingly more efficient in both traditional retail and warehouse/wholesale club outlets.

9. Both companies openly share all appropriate data needed in their joint effort to recognize opportunities for systemic change and improvement. Their attitude is one of trust that each will protect the other in the use of all proprietary information.

The result of this five-year effort is an unprecedented business-building relationship that capitalizes on the common objectives and unique strengths of both Wal-Mart and P&G. They enjoy working with each other in an environment of mutual respect and trust. And in their quest for continual improvement of literally everything they do, both separately and together, the future looks even brighter.

Mirror Team Members

Here's a look at the original mirror team members.

From Walmart

- Logistics—Bryan Banks (team coleader)
- Buying/merchandising—Jim Woodruff, Brent Berry, Don Harris (team coleaders)
- Supply chain—Robert Bruce, Lee Stuckey
- IT—Mark Schmidt, Randy Mott, Randy Salley
- Finance—Butch Jones
- Operations—Don Swann
- HR/people division (involved but not officially on the mirror team)— Suzanne Alford, Marcy Serratt
- Advertising (involved but not officially on the mirror team)—Paul Higham
- Buyers (early counterparts to P&G's group marketing directors, although not officially on the mirror team)—Kirk Hessington, Roger Gildehaus, Dennis Peterson
- Sam's Club—John Freeman, Eddie Frail, Clark Tyndall, Steve Tiernan

From P&G

- Team leader—Tom Muccio
- Product supply—Don Bechtel
- Finance—Kathy Blair
- Store operations—Brad Simpson
- Marketing—Bill Toler
- IT—Mike Graen
- Organization effectiveness—Al Lennon
- Shelf analyst—David Hollenbeck (not officially on mirror team)
- Design team member—John Molter

Customer Team Mission, Vision, and Values

The mission, vision, and values of the P&G-Walmart Customer Service Team were captured nicely in this visual, which was created in 2001, my final year as team leader. It outlines what we wanted the team to look like by 2005.

Visual follows on next page.

MISSION...
something to be accomplished.

The Mission of the Wal-Mart/P&G Business Team is to achieve the long-term business objectives of both companies by building a total system partnership that leads our respective companies and industries to better serve our mutual customer – the Shopper.

What is your role?
Is the direction clear?

We will accomplish our mission through these

STRATEGIES:

Win/Win with Wal-Mart
We will combine and build on the core competencies of Wal-Mart and P&G (Supply/Demand) to accelerate NOS and share growth for both companies.

Create Capability and Capacity
We will efficiently deliver Friday's payroll with excellence while creating increased capacity to deliver breakthrough business results.

Grow Global
We will collaboratively build our global systems and business plans to leverage scale for Wal-Mart and P&G.

VISION...
something to be pursued.

Together, Wal-Mart and P&G have **created a unique** and enduring global **alliance** that combines and builds on the strengths of our two organizations. This synergy has enabled us to improve the lives of the world's consumers, resulting in superior peer group performance and **unparalleled equity growth** for the Wal-Mart and P&G brands.

The Wal-Mart Global Customer Team operates as a **symphony**, which has as its hallmark **breakthrough thinking and performance reliability.**

The Team operates in an environment free of boundaries with each member behaving as a **passionate owner** of the business. The **interactions** of the Team leverage our intellectual capital and diversity, enabling us to perform at our **individual and collective best**, and unleash a passion that drives ever-greater team results.

Are you committed?

Tom Muccio's Personal Operating Philosophy and Expectations

When new hires joined our team, I wanted them to know as much as possible about what we expected, how I tried to lead the team, and what motivations and principles were behind my style of leadership. I created this document and shared it with them so they would have some of those answers and so they could hold me accountable.

1. **Basic beliefs about people**
    - Inherently self-centered and self-seeking and, in general, willing workers.
    - Need vision/purpose that can transcend self, yet mutually co-exist with self-interest.
    - Everybody has opinions and better ideas on most subjects; but, when it comes time to be doers of their word, the crowd dwindles.
    - Identify those around you who are thinkers, doers, owners, and work aggressively to empower them and remove roadblocks from their paths.
    - Credibility (doing what was agreed) is the currency in my economy.
    - Attitude and effort are as important as talent (training can most likely bridge any talent gap).
    - People with bad attitudes (continual negative and disruptive talk and behavior) are cancerous and should be removed.
    - As far as practical, management should be by individual rather than by group.

2. **Personal responsibility/commitment/accountability**

- Authority travels with responsibility and so does accountability.
- A manager is responsible for all that his/her work unit does or fails to do.
- I expect people to own their responsibility area and do whatever it takes to get results within agreed-to control limits.
- Availability of rope will never be the issue, but rather the willingness to recognize and define the expectation, responsibility, and feedback that goes with it.

3. **Autonomy**

- It's there. I expect and want people to use it. If not used productively, it will be restricted individual by individual.
- Believe in risk management—i.e., options, cost, likelihood of success, pro's and con's, contingency plans versus taking chances management.
- Use informal communication/counsel rather than extensive formal reporting and memo writing.

4. **Results orientation**

- Effort, process, and activities are meaningful only if producing the desired *end* results on the expected timeline (i.e., within the control limits).
- We are running a business, and as such our decisions, actions, and priorities should clearly reflect that fact.

5. **Reaction to performance**

- Will always react in the absolute—positively or negatively based on results versus agreed expectations. Then we'll discuss results versus subjective circumstances.
- Reports of bad news should be communicated as quickly as available and should be accompanied by suggestions to improve the immediate situation and followed up with appropriate ideas for system changes in the future.

6. **Recognition, stature, rewards**

- Merit- and results-based journey versus trip time frame.
- Much can be accomplished if you don't care who gets the credit.

- Believe in taking a little more than my share of the blame and a lot less than fair share of the credit. Want people under me to be seen, perceived as the "shooters" in their world.

7. Expectations/information

- Once an expectation is established and agreed, I assume it will happen within control limits unless advised otherwise.
- Early understanding and signaling of variance from expectations indicates "on duty management."

8. Reaction to mistakes

- Minimize harm to business and individual.
- Expect learning and modified behavior as a by-product.
- Much less tolerance with repeated mistakes in same or similar circumstances.

9. Mutual support

- This is a two-way street—we are all customers and suppliers.
- Attitude, credibility, and good informal communication make this happen.

10. Disagreement/dissent

- There is a difference between disagreement and dissent.
- Discussion/disagreement is welcome; it should happen in the open and contain reason, facts, etc. Disagreement unsupported will tend to be resolved upward on significant risks and downward to level of execution in areas of less risk.

11. Additional beliefs

- "Any enterprise is built by wise planning, becomes strong through common sense, and profits wonderfully by keeping abreast of the facts."—Proverbs 24:3,4
- You reap what you sow.
- Trees and people are identified by fruit they produce.

Language Matters—A Glossary of Muccioisms

I t is very difficult for people to relate to complex problems encountered when doing a two-company change where each company has its own embedded language. Creating a visual picture using metaphors helps others to relate to a problem or opportunity. Great metaphors and language can quickly build common understanding and a persuasive case for change. It is the ultimate way to simplify a problem.

Here are some phrases that became known as "Muccioisms" during my time with P&G and that helped keep our team aligned with each other, with P&G team members in Cincinnati and around the world, and with Walmart's team. The list includes more detail about several that are featured throughout the book:

- **A breath mint and a candy mint (or less filling and tastes great)**—Accomplishing two objectives with the same action.
- **A conclusion is the place where you got tired of thinking**—Just because you come up with a great idea doesn't mean you should stop thinking about other, perhaps better, solutions.
- **Bambi in front of a Peterbilt**—Our version of saying someone looked like a deer in the headlights.
- **Building the bike path**—The need to create structures and systems that support success. All organizations are perfectly organized for the results they get.
- **Deep state**—Those who were in power and were quite content with the way things were working. They didn't want to give up authority or risk upsetting their world.
- **Eating the elephant**—Tackling big issues one bite at a time.

- **Encouragement is a free gift; look for opportunities to give it away**—It costs nothing to encourage people, but the return on that action is high.
- **Every day is the Big Game**—This is about bringing your A game to work every day. (The real version is slightly different. Instead of "Big Game" I would use two words that the NFL owns and uses to brand that big game.)
- **Everybody bring a hammer**—When you see something you can fix, fix it. Don't pass it off to someone else.
- **Everyone has a photographic memory. Some just don't have film**—Don't assume everyone remembers what you've told them. Repetition is essential to effective communication.
- **Friday's payroll and invent the future**—The need for short-term excellence in results while also dreaming and testing for the future.
- **Half of the people who are working for you are below average**—A way of helping people understand that if you don't work on the system, you're not going to get the kind of performance you want because all of us are flawed in some respects.
- **If everything seems to be going well, you've obviously overlooked something**—A reminder of the need for constant diligence, renewal, and anticipation of the future. (Alternative: When everything is coming your way, perhaps you're in the wrong lane.)
- **If I need to follow the elephant with a shovel, then I want some input on its diet**—When there was a critical issue with consequences, I wanted to be consulted on it.
- **If the only tool you have is a hammer, everything looks like a nail**—Bring the right tools to the job and don't just pound everything with a hammer.
- **If you want the rainbow, you've got to put up with the rain**—Success comes at some kind of a price, typically inconvenience or the need for courage against pushback. (Alternate versions: If you want to marry the princess, you have to kill the dragon. Or, if you want to marry a prince, you've got to kiss a lot of frogs.)
- **If you want to take credit for the sunshine you need to be responsible for the rain**—A leadership philosophy of taking less credit for the wins and more responsibility for the shortcomings and losses.

- **If your objective is to climb a tree, is it better to train a horse or hire a squirrel?**—I used this occasionally, particularly with the deep state, when trying to get them to add functions and capabilities to the team (as opposed to their encouragement to just have people try harder, work harder, and learn how to do whatever was needed).
- **It starts at the top**—Support from top leaders is critical to the success of any one-company model.
- **It's like a mechanic telling me, "I couldn't repair your brakes, so I made your horn louder."**—My response to the flat-earth society (see "the flat-earth society" below).
- **It's not what you don't know that hurts you as much as what you know that's not so**—Taking actions based on information or expectations that aren't right leads you further and further off course.
- **Learn fast, fix fast, scale fast**—The power of testing and expanding on what you know that works and the return on investment.
- **Many issues call for a both-and solution, not an either-or approach**—It's often easier to go with one solution and shelve other options, but it's usually better to consider ways to try multiple approaches.
- **Moose on the table**—The big problem that nobody wants to talk about or acknowledge.
- **One team, one dream**—A reminder that we were all on the same team working toward a shared vision. People need to know what the end goal looks like, what they are trying to accomplish and why the dream is worth it.
- **Our triune mandate**—The three high-change areas we focused on in the early days of the Walmart-P&G relations: retail formats, categories, and geography. All three areas were growing at a fast rate and at the same time, so they were simultaneously high priorities.
- **Peeling the onion**—As you take off the layers on things you are trying to improve, you might get to something that was even better. The real treasure is often buried three or four layers in.
- **Pictures paint a thousand words**—This is why Jesus taught in parables.
- **Police your area**—We had a lot of conference rooms and held a lot of meetings. My expectation was that when you left a conference room after a meeting, it would be perfectly clean. No coffee cups, soda cans,

and so on. When I left a meeting with my trash, I'd always say, "Police your area," as a reminder that others needed to do the same. That way the next group inherited a clean room.

- **Servant leaders don't think less of themselves, they just think of themselves less**—Wisdom shared with me by Ken Blanchard.
- **Ski on two skis**—Balancing multiple needs at the same time.
- **Stealing ideas from one person is plagiarism, but stealing from many people is considered research**—It's important to look around for better ideas.
- **Swamp**—Bureaucracy and a focus on the status quo.
- **Team members won't care how much you know until they know how much you care**—Leadership team mantra.
- **That was invented when Adam was a lad in the garden; the world is bigger today so let's try something different**—I used this when we had been doing something a certain way for a long period of time and we were resistant to change.
- **The bully meets the maverick**—A reminder that P&G often was seen as a bully in relationships with retail customers, while Walmart had the reputation of a maverick because of its willingness to approach retail in nontraditional ways.
- **The early bird may get the worm, but the second mouse gets the cheese**—Being first certainly has a reward to it, but so does taking something that already exists and making it much better. Everything did not have to be an original idea, and many of the ideas we put into operation came from the design team looking at other industries and other companies to see how they handled problems in similar areas. (Alternative: search and reapply.)
- **The flat-earth society**—Those who resist and reject every new idea because it is different from the current assumption or practice.
- **The pilot's checklist**—You've undoubtedly seen a pilot walk around the plane looking at various things. It may not be enough to stop an accident, but he made sure the basics were reviewed before taking off. I used this analogy to reinforce that every role has a set of important areas that need to be buttoned up on every initiative. It doesn't guarantee the initiative's success, but it does ensure that it doesn't fail for lack of attention and discipline to known potential pitfalls.

- **The problem with incentives is they work**—You get what you recognize and reward.
- **There is a bell-shaped curve of talent and brain power at every level in the organization**—Be prepared to work with a mix of individuals, not just superstars (and remember that in some cases you might not be in an ideal spot on the bell curve).
- **There is no "I" in team**—We have to work together, support each other, and share success to win as a team.
- **Think about how many ways Edison tried before inventing the light bulb**—A reminder not to give up based on Thomas Edison's famous quote, "I have not failed. I've just found 10,000 ways that won't work."[1]
- **Toto, I have a feeling we're not in Kansas anymore**—A line from *The Wizard of Oz* that we used when we discovered something totally new and unexpected.
- **Two in the front**—The secret to driving a two-company change is for both parties to sit in the front seat, looking through the same windshield, with high-beam headlights on so we can clearly see the same road ahead.
- **Walk toward the barking dog**—Problems and tough issues won't go away by ignoring them. Face them and deal with them straight up.
- **Why have a dog and spend a lot of time learning to bark?**—I said this in reference to allowing the people with certain skills and certain functions to make the decisions that were relevant to their functions, rather than having someone who didn't have the background trying to make decisions or influence the way things happen. It's great to question and clarify but, at the end of the day, it's another version of "stay in your lane."
- **You can't have a war story if you don't go to war**—Getting a breakthrough isn't easy. You have to fight the battle.
- **You run cattle but lead people**—My response to those who describe a leader as "he runs" the such-and-such business.
- **You train dogs but develop people**—It's a mindset.

Notes

1. "Famous Quotes by Thomas Edison," Thomas Alva Edison Foundations, accessed April 17, 2024, https://www.thomasedison.org/edison-quotes.

Index

academia, 197. *See also* University of
   Arkansas
accountability, 104, 212
advertising trainees, 76–77
alcohol policy, in Walmart, 93
Alford, Suzanne, 207
American Stores, 20
anti-theft devices, 130
Antonini, Joe, 21–22
ArchPoint Group, 8
Argentina, 190
Arkansas: changes in Northwest region
   of, 53; Fayetteville, author moving to,
   19; P&G team members moving to, 15,
   53–61; Spring River canoe trips in, 27–30;
   Walmart supplier offices in (2023), 4. *See
   also* Bentonville, Arkansas
Artzt, Ed, 37, 121
Arvest Bank Group, 55
Atlanta Bread Company, 112
Australia, 180
Autonomy, 212
awards: Chairman's Club Award, 104, 110,
   111; for failing the team forward, 111,
   147; Vendor of the Year Award, 28–29; in
   Walmart Customer Team, 111

Banks, Bryan, 207
bar codes, 131–32
barking dog metaphor, 125–26, 219
Barkocy, Brian, 83, 149–50, 155
Barren, Brian, 8
bar soaps, 20, 147, 159, 160
Bechtel, Don: on invoice accuracy, 79; on
   meeting with Sam Walton, 4; move to
   Arkansas, 55; on original mirror team,

207; Wal-Mart Customer Team and, 53;
   on Year One Report, 116
Bechtold, Jim, 163
Bentonville, Arkansas, 15; design team's
   visit to, 39–42; looking for office space
   in, 54; P&G multifunctional team offices
   near, 43; visit to Walmart headquarters in
   (1988), 38
Berry, Brent, 149, 190–91, 207
Biddle, Nancy, 58
Billingsley, Boyce, 29
Billingsley, George, 27–28, 29
Blair, Kathy, 40–41, 53, 59, 207
Blanchard, Ken, 201, 218
Blockbuster, 8
Boise Cascade, 182
brand identity, 103
brand managers, 77, 165
brands, private-label, 175–76
Brazil, 190
Breden, Mark, 190
Breissinger, Eric, 8
Brown, Tregg, 8
Bruce, Robert, 8, 207
Built to Last (Collins and Porras), 91
bureaucracy, resistance to change and, 139–40
Bush, George H. W., 37
business partnerships. *See* Walmart-P&G
   partnership
buyer's account, 41

Campbell, Harry: basketball gift to, 111; at
   first office in Fayetteville, Arkansas, 54;
   home in Arkansas, 55; marketing combined with sales under, 75–76; on move to
   Arkansas, 60; promotion of, 109

Canada, 187, 188, 190–91
Carter, Paul, 37, 47, 145
category general managers, 119, 141–42,
   186–87
Cathy, Dan, 107
CEOs: bimonthly meetings with Walmart,
   121; P&G, support for Walmart-P&G
   partnership, 36–37; relationships among
   Walmart and P&G during early years of
   partnership, 37
CFOs, communication among, 121
Chairman's Club Award, 104, 110, 111
change, resistance to. See resistance
Children's Television Workshop, 164
China, 24, 110, 187, 189, 190, 191–92
Christian church, 36, 103
Cifra (Mexican retailer), 189
Cincinnati, Ohio: offices in, 55, 78; Procter &
   Gamble Plaza in, 33; Sam Walton and
   David Glass visiting John Smale in, 33–34;
   Total Quality Management (TQ) seminar
   (1988) in, 34–35
circulars, 134
cleaning supplies, 159, 178, 187
Cleveland Guardians, 8
club stores, beauty products in, 141
Collins, Jim, 91
communication: approaching resistors
   with, 143; differences between P&G
   and Walmart's, 118–19; quarterly and
   monthly letters, 119, 120; through Year
   One Report, 116–18
confidential disclosure agreement, 63–64
Connect to Win, 183
consumer packaged goods (CPG) companies, 132, 181–82, 194–95
consumers: P&G's focus on, 98; shopper
   marketing model, 163–67; shopping for
   good or better, 177; Walmart's commitment to their, 92–94
Continuous Replenishing Program
   (CRP), 78
"correction of errors," 69–70, 88
cosmetics, improving sale of, 156–57
Costco, 141, 179, 182
Coughlin, Tom, 130
courage, of multifunctional team members, 6
Covey, Stephen M. R., 48

cross-functional teams, 4, 5, 15, 19, 140. See
   also mirror team
culture: commitment to an innovative,
   196–97; differences between Walmart
   and P&G, 99, 100; family-like, 107–8;
   patriotism in Walmart's, 94; of Procter &
   Gamble (P&G), 97–99; of rewards,
   147–48; of Walmart, 92–96; Walmart
   and P&G sharing common ground in,
   91–92; of Walmart Customer Team (P&G
   Walmart team), 102–13; Walmart's commitment to customers, 92–94
Currie, Bill, 56, 76
customer business development (CBD),
   109–10, 117, 179–80
customers. See consumers; retail customers

Dallas, Texas, 55, 56, 77
data: point-of-sale, 155–56; products
   shipped to Walmart, 81–82; Retail Link
   and, 83–84, 155; sales, 82–84; sharing,
   82, 83, 87; in Vision of the Future document, 204
"deep state" resistance, 36, 139, 140, 215, 217
Degn, Doug, 24, 96, 130, 135
Deming, W. Edwards, 34
diapers: adding double packs of, 149–50;
   "box-knife damage" of, 129; growing
   category of, 163–65
direct product costing (DPC) data, 204
Dirvin, Gerry, 36–37, 117
disaster relief efforts, 178
displays, store, 145–46
diversity, in P&G workforce, 97–98
Dow Chemical, 140
Dr. John's SpinBrush, 177–78
DSM (science-based company), 183
Dubejsky, Eugene, 190
Duke, Mike, 37–38, 178

Edelman, Jesse, 8; awards of, 111; move
   to Arkansas, 57–58; point-of-sale data
   and, 155
eighteen-month planning cycle, 119, 132
employees: accountability of, 104; diversity in
   P&G's, 97–98; drinking out of Styrofoam
   cups, 33; growth of Procter & Gamble
   (P&G), 186. See also team members

everyday low prices (EDLP) strategy, 159–60
executives: at brand-management seminars by Walmart, 175–76; communication between top, 120; confidential disclosure agreement signed by, 63–64; marketing, 75; P&G culture and, 99; P&G having discussions with other retail, 179; P&G marketing, 75; servant leadership and, 106; servant leadership model and, 106; support for one-company operation model, 117; Walmart, invited to P&G brand management seminars, 175; at Walmart's Saturday morning meetings, 94, 95. *See also* leadership/leaders

failure, rewarding, 111, 147
Faucette, George, 61
Fayetteville, Arkansas: cross-functional team's office in, 15; customer service representatives relocating to office in, 77–78; mirror team meeting in, 13, 65; P&G first office space in, 54
Febreze, 187
Field Agent, 8
Fields, Bill, 8, 39, 157
fiscal year, 25; differences between Walmart and P&G's, 132–33; eighteen-month planning cycle and, 119; Year One Report from first, 116
focus areas, 16, 66, 68, 70
Fortune 500 list, 4
Frail, Eddie, 207
France, 24, 180
Freeman, John, 207
Friday payroll, 169–70, 171, 216

Galloway, Wayne, 22
Gap, 8
Garland, Texas, 185
general managers: P&G category, 119, 141, 186–87; three types of, 23
Germany, 180, 190
Ghoshal, Sumantra, 24
Gildehaus, Roger, 8, 207
Gildersleeve, John, 180
Gillette, 129, 130
Glass, David, 33–34, 86, 95, 121, 140

Glass, Ruth, 37
Gold Club Trophy, 111
"good, better, best" product assortment strategy, 176–77
Graen, Mike, 200; on "comped" prices, 170; at first office in Fayetteville, Arkansas, 54; on mirror team meetings, 65; move to Arkansas and, 60; on original mirror team, 207; Retail Link and, 83, 84; stat cases researched by, 81; on Year One Report, 116
gratitude, 7
Green, John, 155, 202
Greenleaf, Robert, 105
groceries, in Walmart stores, 158
grocery stores, 131, 180

Hardin, Joe Jr., 8
Harding University, 37
Hardy, Arkansas, 29
Harris, Don, 161, 207
Harvest Group, 8
"head, heart, and hands" model for leadership, 201
Henretta, Deb, 165
Hensley, Kim, 59
Hessington, Kirk, 147, 207
Higham, Paul, 207
"high-low" promotion strategy, 127, 128, 150
Ho, Henry: career growth by, 8, 110; in Hong Kong, 190; on quarterly letters, 119; relocating to Arkansas, 77–78; working from Dallas, 55, 77
Hollenbeck, David, 53, 155, 207
hotels: trial-size P&G products sold to, 147–48; Walmart leaders staying in, 34, 93
houses/housing, P&G employees moving to Arkansas and, 54–55, 58
Howell, Dina, 8, 163–65, 166, 167
Hudson Bay Co., 8
humility, 7
Hutchinson, Bill, 47
Hypermarts, 20, 185–86

IBM, 182
incentives, 41, 143, 145–51, 219
Indonesia, 190
initial objectives, 66, 68, 71

innovation/innovation-oriented culture, 98,
99, 149, 161–62, 169, 196–97
Intel, 182
internal design team, 24
international expansion, 151, 180, 181,
188–91
invent-the-future opportunities, 169,
170–71, 216
investor analysis, 85
invoice accuracy/inaccuracy, 79
invoices, P&G product divisions and, 25, 128
Italy, 180

Jacksonville (Florida) Test Team, 22
Jager, Durk, 37
Japan, 180
J. B. Hunt Transport, 59
Jett, Andy, 8, 189, 191
John Brown University, 37, 201
Jones, Butch, 207

Kamp Kia Kima (Boy Scout camp),
27–28, 29
Kent, Ramona, 59
Killingsworth, Pam, 60
Kinko's, 8
Kley, Rich, 155, 190
Kmart, 20, 21, 164, 179, 182
Korea, 190
Kroger, 20, 180

Laco, Tom: quail hunting trip and, 45,
46; support by, 36–37; Total Quality
Management (TQ) seminar and, 34; visit
to Walmart headquarters (1988), 38; VPI
(volume producing item) competition
and, 49
Lafley, A. G.: as CEO of P&G, 23; on reaching customers, 166; support for partnership in early years, 37
Laurer, George, 131
leadership/leaders, 7–8; continuity in PG's,
196; diversity in P&G's, 97–98; face-to-
face communication between, 120–21;
friendships between, 37–38; "head, heart,
and hands" model, 201; importance of
support by, 45–46, 196; international
expansion and, 180, 190, 191–92; P&G,

moving to Arkansas, 55–57; on quail
hunting trip, 45, 46–49; qualities of
Walmart, 95; resistance to innovation
by (see resistance); roles and strengths of
Tom Muccio, 199–201; servant leadership model, 105–8, 201; support for
one-company operating model, 117, 140;
support for Walmart-P&G partnership,
36–37; Walmart and P&G working with
each other, 178; Walmart Customer
Team sharing their story with, 115–21; at
Walmart's Saturday morning meetings,
94–95. See also executives; mirror team;
team leaders
Leahy, Terry, 180
Lennon, Al, 16, 65, 207
letters: author's monthly, 120; quarterly, 119;
from Sam Walton, 63
Lewis, Theresa, 78
Lingardo, Marianne, 79
The Longest Day (Ryan), 102
The Long Walk to Freedom (Mandela), 199
low prices, 14, 77, 83, 93, 127–28, 134, 177.
See also everyday low prices (EDLP)
strategy

Macadoodles, 18
Made in America campaign, 94
Mandela, Nelson, 199
marketing: bringing together with sales,
75–76; P&G co-marketing programs with
Walmart, 163–64; with prebuilt displays,
145–46; shopper marketing concept, 162,
165–67
marketing department, P&G, 75, 76–77,
110, 163
Martin, Bobby, 8, 121
McDonald, Tom, 190
McIlroy Bank, 54–55
McMillon, Doug, 164
meetings: arriving before the start of, 104;
of mirror team, 4, 13, 35, 65–66; Monday
morning huddle (Walmart Customer
Team), 103–4, 107; P&G's design team
and Walmart associates (1988), 39–42;
quarterly face-to-face, 119–20; under
servant leadership model, 106; top-to-top,
121; Total Quality Management (TQM),

34–35; between Walmart executives and John Smale (1987), 33; with Walmart's CEOs, 121; Walmart's Saturday morning, 36, 37, 86, 94–95; Walmart's shareholder's, 84

Merrill Lynch, 25

Mexico, 187, 188, 189

Milligan, Mike, 201; as global head of customer business development (CBD), 179; international expansion and, 180; on multifunctional customer team, 101–2; support for Walmart-P&G partnership, 36–37

Minter, Sharon, 78

mirror team, 4; about, 13, 64–65; career advancement of members, 8; creating reverse bowtie model, 67–68; culture of, 92; end of, 102; exemplifying reverse bowtie model, 67–68; first meeting of (1988), 4, 13, 65; original members, 207; P&G's organizational structure changes and, 73; reviewing operating principles at end of, 71; reviewing opportunities and roadblocks to Walmart-P&G partnership, 16; second meeting of (1989), 13, 16, 19, 65–66. See also P&G-Walmart Customer Service Team

mission statement, 13, 210

Moeller, Jon, 196

Molter, John, 8; expansion with Tesco and, 180, 181; on original mirror team, 207; "proper" breakfast of, 42; Wal-Mart Customer Team and, 53

Montgomery Inn, Cincinnati, Ohio, 34

Moon Pies, 48, 49

Motorola, 182

Mott, Randy, 207

Muccio, Nancy, 19, 35–36

Muccio, Tom, 7, 8; attending Walmart's Saturday morning meetings, 95; career promotions, 110–11; consulting by, 195; as Director, Customer Business Development, 53; faith of, 36; introduction to Sam Walton, 35–36; leadership role, 8; monthly letter from, 120; motivation for work by, 202; move to Arkansas, 19, 55; Muccioisms, Glossary of, 215–19; on original mirror team, 207; Personal

Operating Philosophy and Expectations, 211–13; personal transformation in, 199–202; popcorn talks and, 106; quail hunting trip and, 45, 46–47; resistance personally directed at, 140–41; servant leadership model used by, 106–7; VPI (volume producing item) competition and, 48–49

"Muccioisms," 7, 215–19

multifunctional team(s): expanding into other industries, 183; requirements for P&G, 42–43; research and meetings in Bentonville, Arkansas, 39–43; Tesco/ international expansion and, 180, 181; working with other countries, 189–90. See also one-company operating model; P&G-Walmart Customer Service Team

Murray, Andy, 8, 164

National Underground Railroad, 8

net down pricing, 150

new money, 148–49

NorthStar Partnering Group, 8

O'Brien, Tom, 8

offices: in Cincinnati, 55, 78; P&G culture and, 99; of P&G team leaders, 43; of P&G-Walmart team in Arkansas, 54, 60–61, 103

one-company operating model: approved by John Smale, 179; current relevance of, 196; diagram, 69; expansion of, 179–83; historical significance of, 3–4; imitation of, 19; proposal and response to for test case for, 43–44; reverse bowtie model and, 68, 69; sharing information about, 115–21; support from leadership for, 117, 140. See also Walmart-P&G partnership

OneStone, 8

operating principles, 16, 66, 68–70, 71

operations function, in P&G-Walmart Customer Team, 73, 74–75

Osher, John, 177–78

packaged soap and detergent unit (PS&D), 117

Pampers diapers, 163

Panayotopoulos, Dimitri, 192

Partners in Excellence Award, 63
passion, of multifunctional team, 6
patriotism, in Walmart's culture, 94
Pepper, John, 23–24, 201; on expansion into
    China, 189, 192; friendship with Don
    Soderquist, 37; memo on P&G's customer
    beliefs and strategies (1988), 35; support
    by, 36–37; visiting Walmart headquarters
    (1987), 33
persistence, in multifunctional team mem-
    bers, 6–7
Peterson, Dennis, 207
P&G brands promoted based on everyday
    low prices (EDLP) concept, 159–60
P&G China, 192
P&G Mexico, 189
P&G-Walmart Customer Service Team:
    career growth and opportunities encour-
    aged in, 108–12; continuity in leadership,
    196; continuous replenishment program
    (CRP) and, 77–79; culture of, 92, 100,
    147; Customer Team Mission, Vision, and
    Values, 112, 209–10; developing a unique
    culture of its own, 100; first office for, 54;
    international expansion and, 181; market-
    ing and, 75–77; move to Arkansas, 54–60;
    offices in Arkansas, 54–55, 60–61;
    operations function in, 74–75; original
    team, 53; pathfinders analogy for, 101–2;
    resistance to innovative initiatives by,
    137–43; servant leadership model used
    by, 105–8; unique identity of, 102–5. See
    also multifunctional team(s)
Philippine Association of Supermarkets, 21
Philippines, 21
point-of-sale data, 155–56
Poland, 190
policies, commitment to principles over,
    126–27, 134
popcorn talks, 106
Porras, Jerry I., 91
Portugal, 180
prebuilt displays, 145–46, 150
price points, P&G offering products at lower,
    176–77
prices: competitor promotions and, 169–70;
    "comping" system and, 150; promoted
    products, 134; Walmart's low-price

policy, 93, 96; Walmart versus P&G strat-
    egy for, 127–28
Prilosec, 187
principle over policy approach, 126–27, 134
Pringles, 47–49, 128
Pritchett, Barbara, 29
Pritchett, Lou: after returning from the
    Philippines, 21; bringing marketing and
    sales together, 75; canoe trips with Sam
    Walton, 27–30; George Billingsley and,
    27–28; inquiring into Walmart, 22; meet-
    ing with Kmart CEO, 21–22; quail hunt-
    ing trip and, 45, 46; as "rabble rouser,"
    22; retirement speech, 101; support by,
    36–37; Total Quality Management (TQ)
    seminar arranged by, 34; visiting Walmart
    headquarters (1987), 33; visiting Walmart
    headquarters (1988), 38; VPI (volume
    producing item) competition and, 49;
    on Walmart-P&G relationship before
    partnership, 14
private-label products, 175
problems and challenges: confronting the,
    125–26; damaged goods, 129; in-store
    thefts, 129–31; payment terms, 128;
    pricing strategies, 127–28; prioritizing
    principles over policies when addressing,
    126–27; related to prices of promotional
    specials, 134; related to pricing products,
    127–28; from resistance within P&G,
    137–42; UPC (Universal Product Code)
    errors, 131–32
Procter & Gamble (P&G): alignment of
    business with Walmart, 86–89; CEOs of,
    23; changes to organizational structure
    in, 73–80; consumer packaged goods
    (CPG) companies and, 181–82; culture
    of, 97–99, 101; design team, visit to
    Walmart headquarters, 39–42; dif-
    ferences between Walmart and, 16;
    disaster relief efforts by, 178; diversity in
    leadership, 97–98; fiscal year, 132–33;
    growth in business with Walmart, 4;
    internal design team recommendations
    and research, 22, 23–26, 35; international
    expansion and, 181, 188–91; investor day
    recap from, 85; marketing department,
    75, 76–77, 110, 163; measuring amount

of products shipped to Walmart, 81–82; mirror team members from, 207; multi-functional team from (*see* multifunctional team(s)); new categories of, 186–87; new positions in General Sales Department (1989), 53; partnerships with University of Arkansas, 197; before partnership with Walmart, 13–14, 20; payment terms of, 128; product divisions of (1980s), 20–21, 25; profitability of, improving, 148–49; research on partnerships with retail customers, 22–26; resistance within, 137–42; sales teams, 20–21, 75–76; sharing common ground with Walmart, 91–92; staffing growth, 186; steering team, 23, 24; support by leaders in early years for Walmart-P&G partnership, 36–37; testing facility, 157–58; Vendor of the Year Award and, 28–29; "vision of the future" document of, 26, 203–5; VPI (volume producing item) competition and, 48–49; Walmart store openings and, 188

Procter & Gamble (P&G) Beckett Ridge, 157

Procter & Gamble (P&G) products: acting fast on new items, 160–62; bar soaps, 20, 147, 159, 160; cosmetics, improving sale of, 156–57; damaged, 129; data on sales to Walmart, 82–84; "good, better, best" product assortment strategy and, 176–77; new items, 163; offered at lower price points, 176–77; prebuilt displays for, 145–46; pricing, 127–28; private-label brands, 175–76; product testing for, 98–99; stolen in Walmart stores, 129–31; trading up to better and best, 177; trial size, 147–48; Walmart profits and, 40–42

product divisions, of Proctor & Gamble (PG), 20

profitability, 148–50, 170, 176

profit and loss statements, 93

profits, P&G payment policy and, 40–42

promises, keeping, 173

"promises made, promises kept" motto, 78, 104

promoted products/promotion programs, 204; based on EDLP (everyday low price) concept, 159–60; circulars and, 134; fiscal year and, 132–33; in foreign and domestic markets, 188; "forward buying" and, 127–28; "high-low" strategy and, 127, 128, 150; "invent-the-future" opportunities and, 170–71; protecting the price for, 134; in Vision of the Future document, 204

promotional allowances, 49, 159–60

promotions, employee, 110–11

Puerto Rico, 190

Pūr, 187

Queen City Club, Cincinnati, Ohio, 34

Quinn, Joe, 112

recognition and reward system, 111, 146, 147, 196, 212

resistance, 137–43; from the "deep state," 139; from the "flat-earth society," 139; reasons for, 43, 138; from the "swamp," 139–40

retail customers: customer business development (CBD) teams and, 117, 163, 179; expanding one-company model to other, 179–82; "one-company model" changing how suppliers do business with, 3–4; P&G research and recommendations on relationship with, 24–26; relationship to suppliers, increase in complexity of, 194–95; in traditional bowtie model, 67, 68; understanding of operation of consumer product manufacturers, 24

retailers, P&G acting from position of power over, 20–21

retailer-supplier relationship: essentials for, 197–98; future of, 195–98; increase in complexity of, 194–95; reverse bowtie model, 67–68, 69; traditional "bowtie" relationship, 67, 68

Retail Link, 83–84, 121, 155, 170, 182

return policy, in Walmart stores, 94

reverse bowtie visual, 66, 67

rewards and recognition system. *See* recognition and reward system

RFID (radio-frequency identification) technology, 130–31

Robinson, Kim, 8, 97–98

Russell, Mike, 103–4

Ryan, Cornelius, 102

Saatchi & Saatchi X, 8, 167, 188
sales data, 82–84
sales teams, P&G: marketing brought together with, 75–76; organization of, 20–21
Salley, Randy, 207
Sam's Clubs, 110, 116, 133, 141, 186
Schmidt, Mark, 207
Schomburger, Jeff, 8, 58–59
scorecards, 120, 149
Scott, Lee, 35, 37, 165
Senn, Christoph, 183
Serratt, Marcy, 207
servant leadership model, 105–8, 201, 218
Sherwood, Mindy, 8
Shewmaker, Jack, 37
shoe shining, 107
shopper marketing model, 162, 163–67, 188
Silvestri, Pete, 190
Simpson, Brad, 74–75, 93, 207
Sinek, Simon, 3
sleepovers, 37
Smale, John: allying with Sam Walton, 14–15; introducing author to Sam Walton, 35–36; one-company model approved by, 179; Sam Walton and David Glass visiting (1987), 33; Sam Walton's letter to (1989), 63; support for one-company operating model, 117; Total Quality Management (TQ) seminar (1988) and, 34–35; trip to Arkansas (1988), 36; Vendor of the Year Award and, 28–29
Smale, Phyllis, 35, 36
Smiley, Ella, 59
Soderquist, Don, 37–38, 46, 47, 95, 140, 201
Spain, 180
Spartan Death Race, 15, 16
The Speed of Trust (Covey), 48
Spring River, Arkansas, 27–30
statistical (stat) cases, 25, 81, 83
store managers, Walmart, 74–75
store openings, Walmart, 86, 188, 189
Strategic Account Management Association, 182–83
Stuckey, Lee, 207
SuperValu, 20
suppliers: interest in collaboration with retailers, 181; "one-company model"

changing relationship with retail customers, 3–4; relationship to retailers, increase in complexity of, 194–95; resistance to sharing information with Dow Chemical, 140; in traditional bowtie model, 67, 68
supply chain management, 77, 131
Swann, Don, 207
Swiffer, 187
Switzerland, 183, 190

Target, 179, 182
Team Direct, 8
team leaders, 43; in both Cincinnati and Fayetteville, 56; multifunctional team, 35–36; offices for, in Arkansas, 43; in other countries, 181, 196. See also Muccio, Tom
team members: diversity in, 97–98; encouraging career growth in Walmart Customer Team, 108–12; international assignments, 190; moving to Arkansas, 53–61; new hires of P&G Walmart Customer Service Team, 107–8; onboarding program, 108; rise in positions of, 8; Walmart stock given to, 84–85; working in Walmart stores, 108, 175
team(s): characteristics and values of, 6–7; customer business development (CBD), 109–10, 179–80; diversity in, 97–98; P&G multifunctional, 39–43; research by P&G internal design, 22–26. See also mirror team; P&G-Walmart Customer Service Team
Tesco, United Kingdom, 180–81
testing and test-and-learn practices, 155–62; on groceries in Walmart stores, 158; how to use promotional funds, 159–60; to improve sales of cosmetics, 156–57; P&G facility for, 157–58
Test Team, Proctor & Gamble (P&G), 22
thefts, in Walmart stores, 129–31
ThompsonMurray, 166, 167, 188
Tide, 96
Tiernan, Steve, 207
Toler, Bill, 8, 149; move to Arkansas and, 55–56; on original mirror team, 207; share of Walmart stock, 84–85; Wal-Mart Customer Team and, 53

Toler, Melanie, 55
toothbrush, battery-operated, 177–78
top-to-top meetings, 4, 64, 121
Total Order Management (TOM) system, 78, 80
Total Quality Management (TQ) seminar, 34–35
trial-size products, 147–48
trust: confidential disclosure agreement and, 64; mirror team meetings and, 66, 67, 71; Walmart-P&G journey as exercise in building, 48
Tyndall, Clark, 207
Tyson Foods, 59

uniform communication standards (UCS), 204
United Kingdom, 42, 180, 190
Universal Product Code (UPC) technology, 131–32
University of Arkansas, 53, 59, 111, 166, 186, 197

Valuecreator, 183
values: P&G-Walmart Customer Service Team, 209, 210; team, 6; Walmart and P&G sharing common, 91; Walmart's four basic beliefs and, 92
VCC Associates Inc., 8
Verdery, Tom, 56, 111, 147–48, 159, 190; in Mexico, 190
veterans, military, 94, 97
vision: established at second mirror team meeting, 66; joint determination for bringing to life, 88; of multifunctional team, 6; P&G-Walmart Customer Service Team, 112, 210; Vision of the Future document, 203–5
VPI (volume producing item) competition, 47–49, 128

Wagner, Dennis, 76
Waitsman, Bill, 8
Walker, Julie, 163, 166
Walmart: asking for sales data from, 82; benefiting from partnership model, 197; circulars of, 134; co-marketing program with, 163–65; commitment to custom-

ers, 92–93; "comping" practice, 169–70; consumer packaged goods (CPG) companies and, 181–82; culture of, 92–96; design team's visit to headquarters of, 39–42; differences between P&G and, 16; disaster relief efforts by, 178; doubters at, 142–43; drawbacks of culture of, 96; early recommendation on collaboration with, 26; fiscal year, 132–33; focus on low costs/prices, 93, 96; four basic beliefs/values of, 92; growth of, 194; international expansion and, 188–91; investor analyst meetings, 85; Lou Pritchett inquiring into, 22; measuring amount of P&G products shipped to, 81–82; meetings with CEOs of, 121; mirror team members from, 207; new P&G products and, 161; before partnership with P&G, 5, 14, 20, 22; P&G aligning on business with, 86–89; P&G invoice accuracy and, 79; P&G product testing and, 98–99; pricing strategy, 128; profitability of, improving, 149–51; retail format changes, 185–86; Saturday morning meetings, 36, 37, 86, 94–95; sharing common ground with P&G, 91–92; store operations, 74–75; Total Quality Management meeting (1988) and, 35; on UPC errors, 132; visit to headquarters (1988), 38, 39–42; VPI (volume producing item) competition in, 48–49
Walmart.com, 186
Walmart Customer Service Team. See P&G-Walmart Customer Service Team
Wal-Mart Customer Team, 53
Walmart Hypermarts, 20, 185–86
Walmart Luminate, 84
Walmart Neighborhood Market, 186
Walmart-P&G partnership: author's role in, 199–200; conveying lessons for modern collaborations and business partnerships, 5–7; as game-changing, historical significance of, 3–5; opposition to, 15; resistance to, 137–43; "season" for, 193–94. See also one-company operating model; P&G-Walmart Customer Service Team
Walmart stock, 84–85

Walmart stores: attending first openings of, 86; cosmetics sales in, 156–57; damaged goods from, 129; groceries in, 158; increase in, 187; in Mexico, 189; P&G products and profits of, 40–42; prebuilt displays in, 145–46; promotions and price reductions in, 127; return policy, 94; store openings, 86, 188, 189; team members spending time working in, 175; trial-size P&G products sold in, 147; visits to, 86

Walmart Supercenters, 20, 158, 186

Walton, Bud, 45, 46

Walton, Helen, 28, 29, 35, 36

Walton, Jim, 55

Walton, Rob, 24, 46, 188, 189, 191

Walton, Sam, 201; allying with John Smale, 14–15; on amount of P&G products shipped and sold to, 81–82; on arrogance of P&G sales teams, 21; bird hunting with, 45; canoe trips with Lou Pritchett, 27–30; dog breeding and, 34; early meeting with P&G team member, 4; on Hypermarts, 186; on John and Phyllis Smale, 35;

John Pepper and, 24; letters from, 63; Presidential Medal of Freedom, 37; on priority of the customer, 92–93; on simplicity of Walmart-P&G transaction, 64; thrifty with money, 30; on Total Quality Management (TQ), 34–35; Total Quality Management (TQ) seminar and, 34–35; Vendor of the Year Award and, 28–29; visiting P&G Fayetteville office, 54–55; visit to Cincinnati, Ohio (1987), 33–34; VPI (volume producing item) competition and, 48; on Walmart-P&G relationship before partnership, 14

Walton Institute, 175

Weaver, Anna, 107

Weller, Michael, 183

Witherspoon, Barron, 8, 97–98

Woodruff, Jim, 207

Woolco stores, 187, 188

workforce. See employees; team members

Xerox, 182

Year One Report, 116–18

About the Author

Tom Muccio held many titles in the United States and internationally during his thirty-three years with Procter & Gamble, starting with sales representative in 1970 and ending with President, Special Assignment, in 2003. No matter the other titles, however, he was best known as team leader for the P&G team that established a beachhead for the company in Walmart's backyard and expanded the customer development team concept around the globe.

Tom graduated from Ohio University in 1970 and, after a steak dinner with Bill Parker, Cincinnati District manager for BS&HCP, he took a sales job with P&G. He took on the Walmart team leadership role for P&G in the late 1980s, became a vice president in 1994, and became a president in 2001. In his years after working with P&G, Tom was the CEO for a startup company in Arkansas, and he has stayed active as a consultant and advisor, preaching and teaching many of the principles that led to the P&G team's success.

In addition to his work with P&G, Tom has been a member of the Northwest Arkansas Council, chairman of Arkansas Athletes Outreach, former president of the National Account Management Association, executive director of Compassion Ministries, a board member for Blanchard Training & Development, a board member for Cardone Industries, a member of the CEO forum, a member of the Arkansas Executive Forum, a board member for John Brown University, board chairman of Teen Mania Ministries, a member on the president's advisory council at Bethany University, and a member on the president's advisory board of the American Studies Institute at Harding University.

He and his wife, Nancy, live in Fayetteville, Arkansas, and have two grown children, seven grandchildren, and three great-grandchildren.